THE
MYSTERY TRADITIONS

THE
MYSTERY TRADITIONS

Secret Symbols and Sacred Art

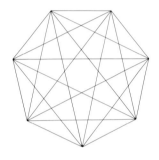

James Wasserman

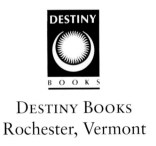

Destiny Books
Rochester, Vermont

Destiny Books
One Park Street
Rochester, Vermont 05767
www.InnerTraditions.com

Destiny Books is a division of Inner Traditions International

Originally published in 1993 by Destiny Books
under the title *Art and Symbols of the Occult.*

This revised edition published in 2005 by Destiny Books
under the title *The Mystery Traditions.*

**The Library of Congress has
cataloged a previous edition of this book as follows:**

Art and symbols of the occult : Images of Power and Wisdom
by James Wasserman
p. cm.
Includes bibliographical references and index.
ISBN 0-89281-415-2 (pbk.)
1. Symbolism.   2. Occultism in art.   3. Symbolism in art.
I. Wasserman, James, 1948–
BF 1623, S9A78   1993
133—dc20   92-38170
                                                                CIP

ISBN of current title *The Mystery Traditions:*
ISBN 1-59477-088-3

Permission to reproduce the many works of art
that appear in this book can be found on pages 146–147.

Book design by Studio 31
www.studio31.com

Printed and bound in China

10 9 8 7 6 5 4 3 2 1

This book is dedicated to the memory of

HARRY SMITH
(1923–1991)

*Master Image Maker,
Teacher, and Friend*

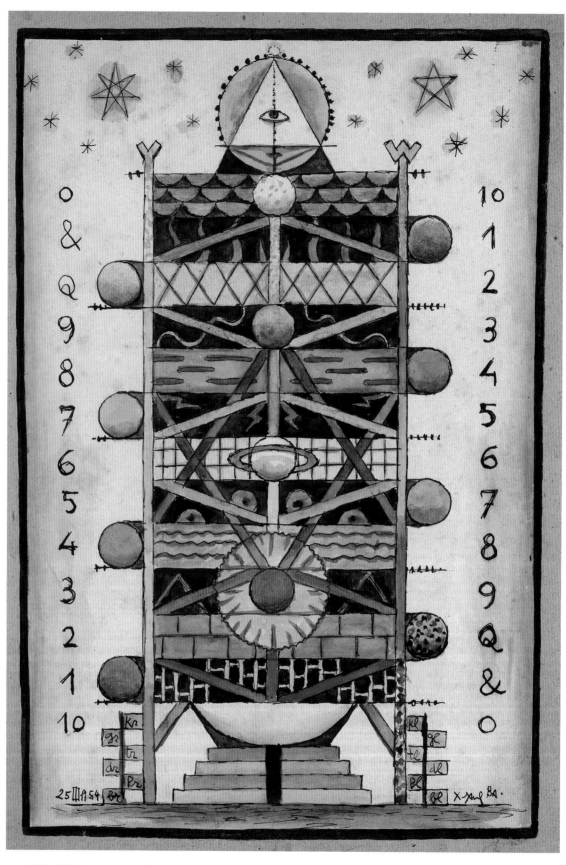

PAN ARBOL (Pan Tree) by Xul Solar, 1954, Watercolor on paper, mounted on cardboard, 35.5 x 24 cm, Museo Xul Solar. Argentinian visionary artist Xul Solar (1887–1963) was a close friend of Jorge Luis Borges who compared him to William Blake. Solar was a personal student of Aleister Crowley and an initiate of the Mystery Traditions.

CONTENTS

Preface to the Second Edition ix

Introduction 1

Astrology and Cosmology 5

Kabbalah and the Tree of Life 21

Initiation 35

Magick and the Gods 55

Secret Societies 71

Sexuality 89

Alchemy 105

Tarot 119

Symbolist and Visionary Art 131

Notes to the Text 141

Suggested Reading List 142

Illustration Permissions 146

THE SUN AT HIS EASTERN GATE (Illustration by William Blake [1757–1827], to Milton's *L'Allegro* 1816–1820) Blake wrote, "The Great Sun is represented clothed in Flames Surrounded by the Clouds in their Liveries, in their various Offices at the eastern Gate."

PREFACE
TO THE SECOND EDITION

*A*SSEMBLING THIS TREASURE HOUSE OF IMAGES IN 1992 for *Art and Symbols of the Occult* was one of the joys of my life. When Inner Traditions offered the opportunity for an expanded edition—to include a new chapter on Secret Societies—it was as if I had been granted a return to that legendary Garden of Delights, flowing with milk and honey and all the many pleasures I so well remembered. For herein are to be found the colors and shapes of the sacred symbols and holy icons that have inspired my own life and that of so many others who have found their spiritual destiny in the Western Mystery Tradition. I have often called this book my visual spiritual autobiography.

The exotic richness of the Western Mystery Tradition is best evoked by its imagery. For in the beauty and symmetry of the holy art of the alchemist, the magician, and the priestess, we are reminded of our indigenous spiritual heritage. Especially in the last five decades, Western culture has been offered a rich infusion of the mysteries and spiritual practices of India, Tibet, China, Japan, and the Arabian peninsula. Simultaneously—yet more gradually—we have been reminded of the spiritual wealth hidden within the formerly subterranean realms of the Mystery Traditions of either over-Christianized or over-Rationalized Europe.

Within the following pages, we will ascend the sacred ladder of initiation in the West. For initiation is the desired result of each of the disciplines explored herein. One studies Astrology to become more conscious of the vastness of the heavens; one practices Alchemy to transmute and purify base matter to its higher essence; the true role of sexuality is to become reflections of, and participants in, the sacred miracle of creation; the roadmap of the Kabbalah charts the ever expanding universe of the psyche; the Tarot is designed to open communication with higher intelligence; the goal of Magick is to become one with the gods; and we are inspired to all this by the visionary record produced by those artists who have made the journey.

Initiation consists in developing experiential awareness of the infinite reach of the soul, and participating in an increasingly intimate union with the Holy. The Mystery Traditions were designed to illuminate the nature of the Divine through initiation. And for many seekers, the natural pathway to initiation includes membership in spiritual secret societies. Thus, in a very real sense, this book has come full circle. In the new chapter on Secret Societies we learn one of the practical ways of reaching our destination.

There are a number of people to thank for the new material in this edition. Once again Hymenaues Beta of O.T.O. shared from the Order's archives, including rare photos of Freida Harris, Jack Parsons, and Aleister Crowley's hand painted lamen design. He introduced me to the work of the Argentine Adept Xul Solar, exposed me to the two paintings by J. F. C. Fuller, and provided recent photographs to replace the two Crowley/Harris Tarot cards in the Magick and Sexuality chapters. Chic and Tabatha Cicero of the Hermetic Order of the Golden Dawn have generously allowed me to present what I believe are the first color images of the most secret and rare Inner Order Temple of the Golden Dawn—for which they have earned the thanks of the entire occult community, as have Donald and Yvonne Weiser who helped to facilitate this opportunity. My friend Dr. Robert Wang offered his dynamic model of the Tree of Life in three dimensions, constructed along guidelines produced by S. L. MacGregor Mathers of the Golden Dawn. George Seghers and Arthur Pierson of the George Washington Masonic National Memorial allowed use of Hattie Burdette's painting of the Father of America in his Masonic regalia. Diane Clements of the United Grand Lodge of England provided the Tracing Board of J. Bowring, a masterpiece of 19th century Masonic iconography. A warm thank you to Diane Cooter at the Syracuse University George Arents Research Library and Jennifer Belt of Art Resource. Curator Patricia M. Artundo and Director Elena Montero Lacasa de Povarché of the Museo Xul Solar went out of their way to help meet a tight deadline for Solar's *Pan Arbol* painting. The members of Swirling Star Oasis—in particular Illia Tulloch—allowed us a rare glimpse of the beauty and symmetry of a properly constructed Gnostic Mass altar. My friends Virlana Tkacz of Yara Arts Group and Joe Kulin of Parabola helped me illustrate the essence of Magick, as I understand it, with the image of Shaman Bayir Rinchinov in ritual communion with higher reality. The brilliant artist and my long time friend Linda Gardner generously allowed me to present one of my favorite paintings as the frontispiece for the Secret Societies chapter. Stella Grey, Bill Thom, and James Strain all made editorial contributions to the new chapter, while Craig Carlisle helped improve the text of the first edition.

A bittersweet collection of personal memories also graces the new pages. I dearly miss Grady McMurtry and Harry Smith. The talented John and Merrie Hodges seem to have died too young and alone for people with such skill. On a joyous note, another soul has chosen the labor and heroism of incarnation since the first edition was published. Our daughter Rachel Tara has been a constant source of inspiration and happiness to both me and her mother, Nancy, who has added the painting of the Solar Greek Cross of the Golden Dawn to the Secret Societies chapter and improved upon our original painting of the Tree of Life, reproduced anew in the Kabbalah chapter. Finally, to Jon Graham, Jeanie Levitan, and the talented staff of Inner Traditions, my sincere thanks once again.

James Wasserman
2005

INTRODUCTION

One must not confuse a symbol with a mere allegory, nor try to see in it the expression of some misty and irrational collective instinct. True symbolism depends on the fact that things, which may differ from one another in time, space, material nature, and many other limitative characteristics, can possess and exhibit the same essential quality. —*Alchemy* by Titus Burckhardt[1]

*T*HE BASIS OF THE MYSTERY TRADITIONS IS *correspondence*. The theory of correspondence recognizes an implicit interdependence of all things with all other things, the existence of multiple relationships between various aspects of Nature's kaleidoscopic richness. Mention the number *six* to a student of the Occult, and you will set off a chain of associations: on the Tree of Life, Beauty and Harmony; in mythology, Solar gods whose nature partakes of resurrection, like Osiris, Ra, Apollo, Adonis, Jesus, Bacchus, and Krishna; in the planets, the Sun; in metals, gold; in perfumes, frankincense; in geometrical figures, the hexagram; in the body, the heart; in the Tarot, the four Sixes and the Princes.

The theory of correspondence is the rationale behind the esoteric teaching that the position of the stars will influence thought, mood, perception, and gestalt. It is the basis of the belief that a cave painting depicting a successful hunt could mysteriously influence the outcome of tomorrow's search for the family's nourishment. It explains why processes performed upon base metals will result in a transformation of the internal psychic structure of the alchemist. It makes possible the leap in understanding necessary to believe that proper sincerity and purity of purpose can influence the apparently random order of shuffled cards, stones, sticks, or tea leaves to form patterns that may be regarded as communication with Higher Minds.

Symbol and image are the alphabet of the theory of correspondence. Man is the Image Maker. This is the major characteristic that distinguishes us from other life forms. It is also the primary characteristic that relates us to Higher Consciousness. Image making is our link, by the theory of correspondence, to divinity. Hermes Trismegistus, the archetypal messenger of divine wisdom, speaks of our power to create images, "you must know, O Asclepius, the power and force of man. Just as the Lord and Father is the creator of the gods of heaven, so man is the author of the gods who reside in the temples. Not only does he receive life, but he gives it in his turn. Not only does he progress towards God, but he makes gods."[2] The human mind must create to live.

The existence of Higher Consciousness is the prime postulate of religion as well as the Mystery Traditions. Myths and legends have developed for millennia to explain the inconceivable fact that Teachers of Wisdom have appeared throughout history to bring the gifts of civilization and spiritual wisdom to a darkened humanity. These Light-bearers have been variously known as gods, angels, spirits, naturally talented geniuses, and extraterrestrial guardians.

Throughout the following pages, the Egyptian religious tradition will be mentioned often and will be referenced as the source of many of the disciplines discussed. Egypt has been called the Mother of Civilization, and it is certainly the birthplace of Western esotericism. The question of how or why the Teaching came to Egypt and left it is beyond the scope of this book. Egypt's fall as a center of wisdom is discernible in a good museum collection by noting the progressive degeneration during the Ptolemaic period. However, the monuments of the earlier dynasties testify to a most exalted Wisdom in both an esoteric and a practical sense. By way of a practical example, Dr. Ogden Goelet, in his introduction to *The Papyrus of Ani*,[3] calculates that if the Great Pyramid were built during the 50-year reign of Khufu (Cheops), the 2.5 million blocks that compose it would have required the placement of one stone (weighing 1.5 tons each) every four minutes, based on a ten-hour workday, seven days a week. The magnitude of this task is even more staggering when one adds the quarrying, shaping, fitting, and delivering of the stones.

The Esoteric Tradition embraces a thoroughly holistic concept of the universe that has been sadly lacking in mainstream Western civilization for the last 2,000 years. Our isolation from Nature has resulted in such havoc that we are threatened with self-extinction as a race. Today an eco-spiritual movement is exploring indigenous cultures in hopes of discovering an integrated worldview in which mankind may participate nondestructively in a recognizable natural order. It is my hope that the awareness of *correspondence,* so aptly demonstrated in the multiple symbols and disciplines of our own Western Esoteric Tradition, as pictured and described in this book, will help to stimulate a level of consciousness conducive to the self-preservation of humankind. I believe that the celebration of the intellect, a unique component of Western thought, may allow this to take place without a return to the stone age technology often suggested as the means to accomplish it.

I wish to acknowledge the following people who have added so much to this project. First and foremost my thanks go to Sean Konecky, who contributed the chapter on Visionary Art. His patient and painstaking editing constantly challenged me to produce the best work I could. Nancy Wasserman cheerfully accepted life in an obsessive universe for many months. Her editorial/production skills and artistic contributions have enriched this book immeasurably. Paula Wechter's well-organized, intelligent, and tenacious energy in the Herculean task of handling permissions was absolutely critical. Thanks are also due to Michael McCarthy of W. S. Konecky; Henry Suzuki, Don Rifkin, Sean King, and the staff of Weiser's Bookstore; Donald Weiser and Betty Lundsted of Weiser Publishing; Art Kunkin and Alice Buse of Philosophical Research Society; Stuart Kaplan of U.S. Games; Hymenaeus Beta of Ordo Templi Orientis; Martin Starr of Teitan Press; Pat Kilgore of Giant Photo; and Don Snyder of Precision Guesswork Program. Special thanks are due to Ehud Sperling and Leslie Colket of Inner Traditions International for providing essential thematic direction and making this book possible. Finally, thanks to my mother and father, and to my son, Satra.

Fall Equinox, 1992
New York City

OPPOSITE: THE PORTAL OF THE OUTER ORDER (Painting by J. F. C. Fuller, 1909)
The Candidate prepares to take her first steps upon the Path of Initiation.

ASTROLOGY
AND COSMOLOGY

Astrology is the study of the heavens and their relation to life on earth. It was originally the science of astronomy. During the late 17th century, however, science developed an empirical imperative and based its activities on strictly rationalistic data. While the spirit of skeptical inquiry helped to free science from older superstitions, some of the richness of the knowledge of earlier civilization was lost in the process. Modern 20th century discoveries in physics have forced science to correct its embrace of what might accurately be described as the superstition of hyperrationalism.

Although there may be general disbelief that the patterns of the heavens can in any way contribute to consciousness here on earth, certain planetary effects on terrestrial life are undeniable. For example, the effect of the moon on the tides is a scientific fact; the relationship between behavior of the mentally ill and the occurrence of the full moon is statistical; and the moon's relation to the female menstrual cycle is incontrovertible. (Not surprisingly, in Astrology, the Moon governs feelings, emotions, and the rhythmic tides of the subconscious.) What science may eventually be able to measure of the more subtle effects of the celestial realms on life on earth remains to be seen.

The Roots of Astrology

To ancient man, the heavens symbolized the home of the highest gods. Night and day were controlled therein. Storms, lightening, thunder, and eclipses were recurrent reminders of the enormous power of Nature symbolized by the sky. The vastness of its reach demonstrated its all-containing nature. Filled with stars at night, the sky suggested to the ancients a woman bending as if to suckle the babe earth.

MILKY WAY STAR CLUSTER IN THE CONSTELLATION OF SAGITTARIUS

The sacred sciences all evolved from a study of the heavens. Early man searched for signs of order in a chaotic world. Scientific sky watching became a primordial survival skill. Regular and recurrent cyclical patterns were measured and such lore was handed down from generation to generation in all corners of the earth. Man became able to predict the seasons. This knowledge allowed for more efficient hunting and agricultural pursuits.

The annual journey of the sun, apparently circling the earth in 365 days, was duly noted. The phenomena of the solstices (the longest day of the year in summer and the shortest day in winter) and the spring and fall equinoxes (when day and night were of equal length) would lend to the year a sense of quadrature. Crosses and circles, expressing these observations, became the earliest abstract graphic symbols. The laws of Nature were astrological laws.

Myths and fables began to develop, populating the sky with powerful beings who influenced and controlled the lives of human beings and the events on earth. The world was understood to be ruled by these entities, grouped in similar hierarchies in culture after culture. The similarities are more profound than the differences. The legends grew to become more accurate, intricate, and defined, and this process continues to our own day.

As agriculture became predominant and people and tribes remained in one area for long periods, temples would be erected to honor the gods and beings whose powers were so important. Calendars were developed that charted the annual rhythm of the sun and the monthly rhythm of the moon. Names were assigned to months and days. Festivals and religious observations were timed to coincide with these recurrent patterns, to propitiate the deities and to celebrate and honor their deeds.

Astronomers were the priests, the keepers of records, the compilers of the calendar, the repositories of the myths, and the organizers of worship. They assumed even greater power within the community as their researches became more relevant to the survival of the group. Their ability to predict natural phenomena, based on analysis of records and personal observations, could make the difference between life and death.

These developments took place over thousands of years. The celestial components of the resulting astrological system include, primarily, the Planets, the Signs of the Zodiac, the Houses, and the Aspects. These components are charted, and their relationships are analyzed, in star maps called Horoscopes. We will briefly explore here the basics of Astrology; the interested reader is referred to the suggested reading list for further study.

THE PLANETS

The ancients identified the seven planets visible to the naked eye with seven planetary gods. The word *planet* comes from a Greek root meaning "wanderer." The motion of the planets differed dramatically from that of the fixed stars. They were associated with free spirits who ruled and directed the course of earthly events below. Sun and Moon are the two most intimate planets in their relationship with Earth. They form the archetypal couple, bride and bridegroom, mother and father of the human race. In the Greek pantheon, most familiar to our Western culture, the planets were identified as follows: The Sun is the Greek Apollo, Lord of the Day and symbol of the light of consciousness. The Moon is Diana, Lady of Night and the sensuous subconscious. Venus is Aphrodite, Goddess of Love and luxury. Mercury is Hermes, identified as the archetypal Messenger. Mars is Ares, the God of War and strength. Jupiter is Zeus, the father of the gods and ruler of the heavens. Saturn is Chronos, the time warden and Lord of Discipline.

Neptune, Uranus, and Pluto, invisible to the naked eye, were discovered much later through the use of the telescope. Modern Astrology assigns Neptune to inspiration and ideals; Uranus to the unexpected and innovative; and Pluto to major transformation and power.

THE SIGNS

The signs of the Zodiac derive from observation of the apparent path of the sun around the earth through the year. There are at least two ways of looking at the heavens. In the first, the *geocentric* view, the sun and constellations are described as moving around the earth. This corresponds to how they appear to our senses as we watch the sky at sunrise, noon, sunset, and through the night. The geocentric view is the basis of most forms of Astrology. The second view is the *heliocentric*, which correctly concludes that the earth revolves around the sun. The heliocentric system was taught by Aristarchos of Samos (ca. 320–250 B.C.E.). Aristotle wrote that Pythagoras (ca. 600 B.C.E.) also taught that the sun was the center of a circle around which the earth traveled. Copernicus (1473–1543) revived these earlier beliefs.

The equator is an imaginary circle around the center of the earth, dividing it in half between North and South. (See diagram.) This circle, extended into space, is called

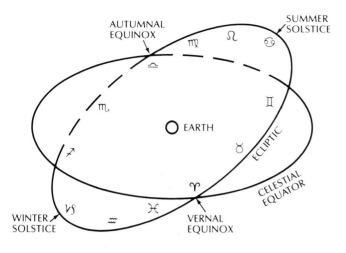

DIAGRAM OF THE ECLIPTIC AND CELESTIAL EQUATOR

the *celestial equator*. The apparent path of the sun through the year "around the earth" is called the *ecliptic*. The intersection of the ecliptic with the celestial equator occurs in two places that mark the spring and fall equinoxes. The northernmost point the sun reaches along the ecliptic marks the summer solstice; the southernmost point, the winter solstice. Moving along the band of the ecliptic, which is about 16 degrees wide, is a group of fixed stars apparently encircling the earth. The sun appears to pass through them in its annual pilgrimage. The ancients grouped these stars into imaginary units called constellations, which are the 12 zodiacal signs of Astrology. The word *Zodiac* is from a Greek root and means "circle of animals." The 12 constellations, or signs of the Zodiac, are traditionally assigned characteristics, which they are said to impart to persons or events born on earth while their influence predominates.

Aries, the Ram, injects the initial surge of energy and dynamic creativity at the spring equinox. *Taurus,* the Bull, stabilizes and builds upon the energy. *Gemini,* the Twins, activates it on a mental plane. *Cancer,* the Crab, imparts a fructifying, feminine, lunar quality, whereas *Leo,* the Lion, provides the male solar heat. The successful alchemical transformation undergone by the Sun during its passage from the feminine Cancer to the masculine Leo is said to be the basis of manifestation. *Virgo,* the Virgin, adds analytical mental awareness and discrimination. *Libra,* the Scales, balances all these qualities and adds the dynamic of relationship. *Scorpio,* the Scorpion, announces the death of the year and the accompanying implicit psychic and intuitive awareness of rebirth. *Sagittarius,* the Archer or Centaur, provides the reflective philosophical perspective as the turning inward of winter begins. *Capricorn,* the Goat, the young

solar god born at the winter solstice in uncounted traditions, marks the emergence of the Sun from the darkness and death of the longest night of the year. *Aquarius,* the Water Bearer, introduces social consciousness and the awareness of higher ideals. *Pisces,* the Fishes, psychic and reflective, internally directed at the end of the cycle, provides the dark womb and dampness from which the fiery Aries may burst forth once again.

THE HOUSES

The houses are another important constituent of Astrology. They are determined by the earth's rotation around its axis on a diurnal or daily basis. The 12 constellations of the Zodiac are empowered daily for approximately two hours each as measured at the equator. There are several different systems for calculating the houses; however, they all share in common the determining of the constellation on the horizon at the moment of birth, called the rising sign or ascendant.

The houses influence the basic areas of life in the following manner: The *first* house, the rising sign or ascendant, rules the appearance and manner in which one presents oneself to the world. The *second* house rules finances, career, and resources. The *third* rules communication, short trips, and immediate surroundings. The *fourth* concerns the home, family, childhood, and the mother. The *fifth* house rules pleasure, creative self-expression, sex, and children. The *sixth* rules work, service, and health. The *seventh* house concerns partnerships and alliances. The *eighth* concerns legacies, death, and rebirth. The *ninth* rules philosophy, education, and self-enrichment. The *tenth* house rules career, long-range goals, and the father. The *eleventh* concerns friends, group activities, and humanitarian interests. The *twelfth* rules the occult, hidden influences, and the subconscious mind.

It should be noted that the signs and houses are aspects of each other, symbolic of the same energy in different areas. Thus Aries corresponds to the first house, Taurus to the second, and so on. The signs are more personal; the houses, more general. Such fluidic interrelations of symbols occur throughout the Esoteric Tradition.

ASPECTS

The fourth major component of an astrological chart is the relationship between the planets measured by the angles they form to one another. The horoscope is a 360-degree circle. When two planets are in signs that have a mathematical angular relationship, they are said to influence each other's sphere of activity on the basis of that angularity. The major aspects include *Conjunctions* (0-degree angles), which cause planetary energies to join, combine, or blend. *Sextiles* (60-degree angles) cooperate with, help, and ease. *Squares* (90-degree angles) challenge, test, or, irritate. *Trines* (120-degree angles) harmonize and energize. *Oppositions* (180-degree angles) balance, oppose, and confront. For example, Cancer and Capricorn are in opposition; Aries and Leo in trine. If in a particular chart the sun is in Cancer in opposition to the moon in Capricorn, within, say, 5 degrees of orb, there would be a tension between the conscious will and the unconscious mind.

THE FOUR ELEMENTS

As we progress through the study of various areas of occultism, we repeatedly come across the division of energy into three and four. The 12 signs are divided into four elements, corresponding to *Fire, Water, Air,* and *Earth.* These elementary energies correspond to their physical counterparts only in the most general symbolic way. For example, Fire is active and energetic; Water, reflective and sensual; Air, nimble and agitated; Earth, stable and practical. The three Fire signs are Aries, Leo, and Sagittarius. The Water signs are Cancer, Scorpio, and Pisces. The Air signs are Gemini, Libra, and Aquarius. The three Earth signs are Taurus, Virgo, and Capricorn.

THE THREE QUALITIES

The zodiacal signs are also grouped into divisions called *Cardinal, Fixed,* and *Mutable.* The Cardinal signs represent an original creative energy within the element group; the Fixed signs represent a sustaining or passive energy; the Mutable signs act as a connecting or change-producing force. One sign from each elementary group is assigned to one of the three triplicities. The Cardinal signs are Aries, Cancer, Libra, and Capricorn. The Fixed signs are Leo, Scorpio, Aquarius, and Taurus. The Mutable signs are Sagittarius, Pisces, Gemini, and Virgo.

DIGNITY

When the planets are passing through the zodiacal signs, their influence can be either strengthened or weakened according to their relationship to the energies of the sign. This relationship is called Dignity and is analyzed in four categories: *Rulership, Exaltation, Fall,* and *Detriment.*

Rulership refers to signs and planets that most nearly correspond to one another. Exaltation is enhancement of planetary qualities by the sign. A planet in the sign opposite its Rulership cannot express itself well and is in its Fall. A planet in the sign opposite its Exaltation is frustrated in its activities and hence in its Detriment.

THE HOROSCOPE

The horoscope is an exact representational picture of the position of the heavenly bodies at any given moment. The most generally familiar is the natal horoscope, which depicts the heavens at the moment of birth when viewed from the exact location of the event. A chart can also be cast for the day of a proposed act and viewed for favorable or unfavorable influences on the venture.

The theory of correspondence actually begins with the particularizing of the universal in Astrology. The ancient world viewed the human being as an integrated whole, as a functioning microcosm, or small world, of the greater or macrocosmic universe. The study of the heavens led to the conclusion that man and woman reflect the heavens by analogy.

Astrology gave rise to psychology. Astrologers studied the heavens and taught that the data thus gathered were applicable to the inner workings of the human being. A person's tendencies could be elucidated by an understanding of the cosmic forces active in his or her life and birth. One could also rebalance planetary influences for psychological healing through the use of magical imagery. For examples of such archetypal designs, see pages 10 and 11.

The ancients also believed that our internal organs correspond to the planets and signs of the cosmos. (See pages 9 and 24.) Healers could diagnose illnesses on an astrological basis and prescribe the herbs associated with corrective planetary activity (by the theory of correspondence) to heal their patients. This might involve either stimulating or inhibiting a planetary function. Hippocrates, the father of modern medicine, said that a doctor who did not use Astrology to aid in diagnosis and choice of remedy was more a fool than a physician.

In the images presented here, a vision of wholeness emerges. The Circle always represents completion. The Zodiacs from different cultures and times resemble not only each other but mandala art generally. Something more than a mere map is presented in a zodiacal chart or horoscope. The symbols point the way to the psychic integration of the individual Self with the universal Will, otherwise known as the Great Work of Adeptship.

ZODIACAL FIGURE (Manuscript illumination by the Limbourg Brothers, *Trés Riches Heures du duc de Berry,* early 15th century, France) A Book of Hours is an almanac that relates seasonal activities and celestial motion to biblical passages and specific prayers. *The Zodiacal Figure* beautifully illustrates the iconographic images of the astrological signs within the months of the year. It also shows the parts of the body they control. See page 24 for another version.

CLOCKWISE FROM LEFT: PLANETARY SEALS
(Manuscript illuminations, *De Sphaera*, 15th
century, Italy) The seven holy planets, visible to
the naked eye, include the Moon, Venus,
Mercury, Mars, Jupiter, Saturn, and the Sun. This
beautiful series of miniatures shows the magical
image of each planet and the two zodiacal signs it
rules, except in the case of the Sun and Moon,
which each rule only one sign. The Renaissance
fascination with planetary images derives from the
research of that time into the ancient theurgic
practices of invoking planetary energies to
develop the psyche. Each planet is regarded as
the source and incarnation of specific energy
patterns: for example, Mars connotes strength;
Mercury, intelligence; Jupiter, wealth; and so
forth. The system of magical images allows for
visual concentration on specific archetypes.

ADORATION OF THE LAMB (Manuscript illumination, *Commentary on the Apocalypse*, by Beatus of Liebana, ca. 970 C.E., Spain) "... behold, in the midst of the throne and of the four living creatures, and in the midst of the elders, a Lamb" (Revelation verse 5:6). St. John's description of the celestial court has been beautifully adapted to suggest a zodiacal theme. (Compare this illustration to the Jewish Zodiac on page 15.) The position of the Lamb indicates the Sun; the four living creatures, the quadrature of the year in the Solstices and Equinoxes. There are twelve positions around the circle (although there is a greater number of figures), suggesting the zodiacal signs.

OPPOSITE: ASTROLOGER STUDYING THE ZODIAC (Manuscript illumination, 15th century, France) This medieval Astrologer is shown in his observatory, situated in the center of a circle. The circle encloses a dodecagon, formed by the intersecting lines originating from the zodiacal signs distributed around its circumference. He appears to be holding a star chart against the sky.

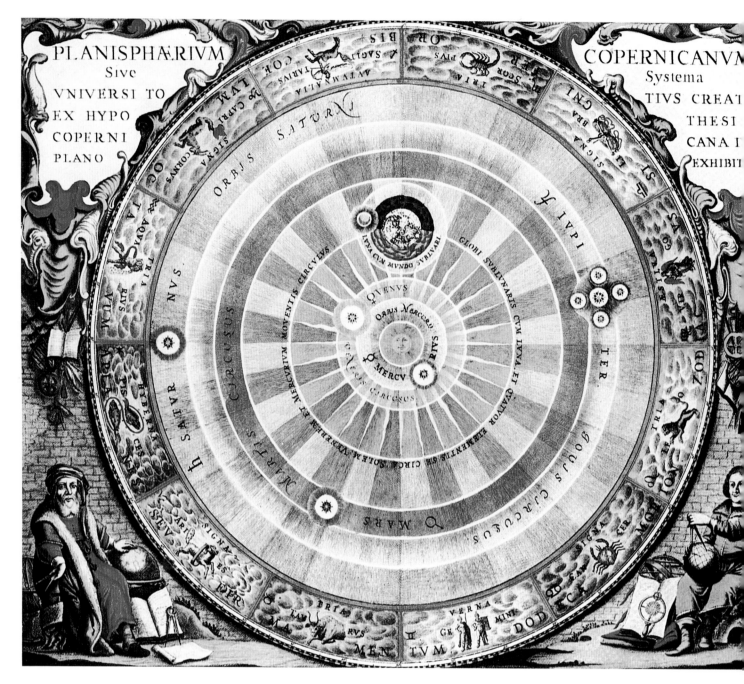

COPERNICAN PLANISPHERE (Engraving by Andreas Cellarius, *Harmonia Macrocosmica,* 1708)
There is a sense of triumph in the coloring and layout of this scientific design. The heliocentric system heralded a return to the ancient mysteries entertained by Renaissance hermeticists. Buried for centuries in forgotten byways, the heliocentric worldview was seen as a restoration of ancient light in a world of modern darkness. Copernicus, although basing his theory on mathematics, acknowledged ancient sources and even quoted Hermes Trismegistus in his development of the heliocentric theory.

OPPOSITE ABOVE: DENDERAH ZODIAC (Drawing by artists of the Napoleonic expedition, ca. 1799, with color scheme by Alden Cole, 1978) The Zodiac was on the ceiling of the Temple of Isis at Denderah on the east bank of the Nile. It is said to represent midnight of the summer solstice, 700 B.C.E., when Sirius rose at dawn with the sun. The orientation of the temple suggests that on that day, as beams of light from the star shone through the temple door, rows of carefully spaced columns focused the light until it illuminated the Altar in the Holy of Holies.

OPPOSITE BELOW: MOSAIC PAVEMENT (Beth Alpha Synagogue in Northern Israel, 6th century) This mosaic of the Hellenistic period represents the Sun, personified as Helios on his chariot. He is surrounded by the 12 zodiacal signs. The four figures at the corners personify the four seasons.

EMPYREAN HEAVEN (Illustration by Ebenezer Sibly, *A Key to Physic, and the Occult Sciences* by Ebenezer Sibly, 1794) Sibly describes his design as "A plate of the interior heaven, with the different orders of the Spirits and Essences of the Divine Mind, distinguished by their proper names and character. It will also appear from this plate, in what manner the rays or beams of Divine Providence pass from the center or seat of Godhead, to all the different orders of the angels and spirits to the *Anima Mundi,* and thence to all the celestial bodies, planets and stars; to our earth, and to the remotest parts of infinite space." The fall of Lucifer is shown near the center. The figure is based on a design by Heinrich Khunrath.

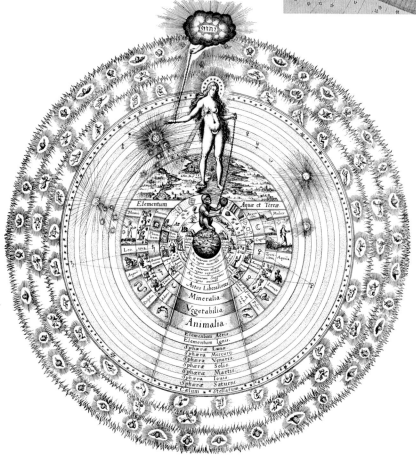

THE MIRROR OF THE WHOLE OF NATURE AND THE IMAGES OF ART (Engraving by Johannes de Bry, *Utriusque Cosmi Majoris . . .* by Robert Fludd, 1617) This magnificent drawing depicts the Animal, Vegetable, and Material worlds; the worlds of Earth, Air, Water, and Fire; the Planets; and the Heavens. Nature is shown as a beautiful naked virgin governing through her dependence on God Above, *IHVH,* holding the chain to her right wrist. She is the source of feminine creativity. The Ape of Nature is her helper, the human world, holding the end of the chain that extends from Nature's left hand. Around the inner circle are the Arts and Sciences.

ATLAS BEARING THE HEAVENS (*Coelifer Atlas*, Woodcut, 1559) This geocentric diagram of the heavens includes the planets, enclosed within the zodiacal band. The earth is the center of the celestial sphere. The celestial equator is shown, as are the poles. The four elements influence the earthly sphere. The banner is a partial quote from Vergil's *Aeneid,* I:742–743. As it appears above, it reads, "Here he will sing of the wandering Moon and of the eclipses of the Sun and of Arcturus and the rainy Rainers and the twin Ploughers." (Arcturus, Rainers [Hyades], and Ploughers [Triones] are star names.)

ALMANAC FOR JUNE (Manuscript illumination by the Limbourg Brothers, *Trés Riches Heures du duc de Berry,* early 15th century) This plate shows the month of June, the period of Gemini and Cancer. On the left are the twins of Gemini, and on the right is the crab of Cancer. In the inner circle the sun god is shown astride his chariot drawn by winged steeds. The numbered days of May and June are on the outside rim. Lunar phases are given in the inner semicircle along with sun risings. The workers in the realistic scene below demonstrate the seasonal agricultural activity of this time of the year. The still extant Sainte Chapelle church in Paris is shown on the right.

STONEHENGE (Idealized painting of a historical ceremony. *The Costume of the Original Inhabitants of the British Islands* by Sir Samuel Rush Meyrick and Charles Hamilton Smith, London, 1815) Numerous legends have grown around the origins of Stonehenge—itself a form of almanac. Present day archaeology asserts that it was built gradually, beginning before 3000 B.C.E. Numerous theories assert that Stonehenge was, not only a temple and ancient burial ground, but also an astronomical observatory and almanac, keyed to the summer solstice, much like the Temple of Denderah shown on page 15. Intricate astronomical computations for determining solstices, equinoxes, sunsets, sunrises, moonrises, and eclipses can be derived from the relative position of the stones and their proportions.

GRAND MAN OF ZOHAR (Illustration by J. A. Knapp, *The Secret Teaching of All Ages* by Manly P. Hall, 1925)

KABBALAH
AND THE TREE OF LIFE

*T*HE KABBALAH MAY BE DEFINED as the esoteric Jewish doctrine. The word "Kabbalah" comes from the Hebrew root *QBL,* meaning "to receive," and refers to the passing down of secret knowledge through an oral transmission.

The Kabbalah is said to have been taught by God to a select company of Angels in Paradise who then conveyed it directly to Adam, after the Fall, as a means for him to reclaim his former spiritual grace. It was passed on to Noah and then to Abraham. Abraham traveled to Egypt, where he shared the doctrine with priests who taught it to other nations. Moses himself was first initiated in Egypt and became adept in the Kabbalah during his desert wanderings, where he was also taught directly by the Angels. Moses concealed the doctrine within the first four books of the Pentateuch. This accounts for the importance placed on biblical analysis within the Kabbalah.

The teaching remained deep within the Jewish culture until Rabbi Simeon Ben Jochai's disciples collated his treatises into the central kabbalistic work, the Zohar. Rabbi Simeon Ben Jochai lived during the 1st century. The Zohar is the record of discussions with his son, conducted during the 12 years they hid in a cave after the Roman Emperor had sentenced the great Rabbi to death for criticizing the Empire. The collection of mystical kabbalistic doctrine was first published in Spain in the 13th century. (In oral traditions, the dating and authorship of early written documents are often obscure and may become the subjects of scholarly examination and contention.)

Such is the legendary derivation of the Jewish Kabbalah. A kabbalistic tradition exists as well in the Arabic and Greek languages. Some authorities say the Kabbalah originated in Egypt. Egyptian sacred art exhibits a correspondence between the postures of figures in its vignettes and the shapes of hieroglyphics. Initiates of the Mysteries would learn the secret keys that allowed them to decode these symbols.

The evolution of Kabbalah into a more widespread force in European esotericism took place in the Middle Ages, when the Jewish Kabbalah entered Christian consciousness through the works of Pico della Mirandola (1463–1494). Thus was developed the Hermetic Kabbalah, the marriage of Greek Hermeticism and Jewish Kabbalah. Pico's interest, inspired perhaps by unpublished manuscripts of Raymond Lull (1235–1315), influenced Cornelius Agrippa (1486–1535), Robert Fludd (1574–1637), and many others who were deeply versed in the Kabbalah and who directly or indirectly influenced the Rosicrucian flowering during the 16th and 17th centuries. In the mid-19th century, Eliphas Levi popularized kabbalistic doctrines in his widely read books. In the latter part of the 19th century, Kabbalah was adapted as the primary symbolic language of the Hermetic Order of the Golden Dawn through two of its founders, William Wynn Westcott and S. L. MacGregor Mathers. The resulting 20th-century development was affectionately called "bop kabbalah" by Allen Ginsberg in his epic elegy, *Howl*.[1]

The theory of correspondence thoroughly informs the Kabbalah. The primary symbolic groupings within the tradition are the division into Four, the division into Ten, and the division into Twenty-two.

THE FOUR WORLDS

The structuring of reality as we perceive it is patterned after the Divine Name *IHVH* (Jehovah). Each letter of the Name is assigned to one of the Four Elements: Fire, Water, Air, and Earth, respectively. The four elements are the primary "qualities" with which the amorphous and purely "quantitative substance" of all physicality first enters differentiated form.

The letters *IHVH* also refer to the four Planes of Reality called the Four Worlds. These include *Atziluth*, the Archetypal World, or world of pure idea, the root-notions and volition behind all form; *Briah*, the Creative World, in which are contained all patterns of general ideation; *Yetzirah*, the Formative World, the world of thought, imagination, and specifics of individual design, the astral plane; and finally *Assiah*, the Material World, or tangible manifestation of these finer levels.

THE TREE OF LIFE AND THE THIRTY-TWO PATHS OF WISDOM

The most important graphic symbol of the Kabbalah is the Tree of Life. It is a richly provocative image, the ultimate symbol of creation; all of nature is included in its schema. As a visual diagram it is composed of ten spheres, or *Sephiroth*, and 22 Paths connecting the spheres. It may be seen in color on page 28 and with the traditional attributions on page 29. The ten spheres represent the numbers from one to ten, and the 22 paths correspond to the 22 letters of the Hebrew alphabet. Together they are the 32 paths of Wisdom described in the *Sepher Yetzirah*, an early kabbalistic text attributed to Abraham. The learned Kabbalist Rabbi Aryeh Kaplan[2] states that if Abraham were the author, the work would date from around 1800 B.C.E., about the same time as the Vedas. The Egyptian Books of the Dead were also contemporaneous. The *Sepher Yetzirah* is generally acknowledged as having appeared in writing about the 1st century.

THE TEN NUMBERS

The Kabbalah includes a numerical description of the successive emanation of our known universe from the nothingness prior to creation. The unfolding of reality through number was resumed by Aleister Crowley in a treatise entitled the "Naples Arrangement,"[3] on which the following discussion is based. The essential question is this: How do we understand manifestation in its most basic terms? (It will be helpful for the reader to refer to the Tree of Life diagram on page 29.)

The progressive emanation of the physical world described as a mathematical sequence begins with the number Zero, called in the Kabbalah, *AIN* (Nothing), the Primordial Void. Within *AIN*, the Kabbalists conceived of something similar to Infinite Space, which they called *AIN SOPH* (Without Limit). They further postulated *AIN SOPH AUR* (The Limitless Light), akin to the space–time continuum. These concepts, thoroughly abstract, establish the preconditions of physical manifestation. They are known as the Triple Veils of the Negative.

ONE: Manifestation begins with the the Point, the number One (*Kether*—the Crown), the idea of Position. It has neither parts nor magnitude. It is positive, yet indefinable because it has no relation to any other manifested idea.

TWO: The Point becomes the Line, the number Two (*Chokmah*—Wisdom). Now we can define the Point as at least distinguishable from one other; yet the Line cannot include measure unless there is a third reference.

THREE: This brings us to the Triangle, the number Three (*Binah*—Understanding). We can define and describe the three points in relation to one another. For example: "A is nearer to B than to C."

THE ABYSS: The Triangle has introduced the idea of surface, the Plane. Here is an Ideal World of Forms, still without substance or solidity. The Plane of the Triangle must remain an imaginary world forever unless something occurs to continue the process of progressive manifestation. This leap from the Potential to the Actual is symbolized in the Kabbalah by the imaginary Sephira, *Daath* (The Abyss).

FOUR: Thus comes the Solid, the number Four (*Chesed*—Mercy). Now there are three coordinate axes—North and South, East and West, Above and Below. The original Nothingness of *AIN* has finally become Matter.

FIVE: The situation, however, is still tenuous, because nothing can "happen." In the analysis of reality as we perceive it, we must postulate a fifth positive idea, Time (which implies Motion), the number Five (*Geburah*—Severity).

SIX: Now the Point can experience a Past, Present, and Future. It has finally attained Self-Consciousness, which is the number Six (*Tiphareth*—Beauty).

SEVEN: Self-Consciousness develops an awareness of the three basic qualities of existence that the Point must possess to have a sensible experience of itself. The first quality is the Emotional Nature (Bliss), the joy of existence that impels the soul to embrace incarnation despite suffering. This is the number Seven (*Netzach*—Victory).

EIGHT: The second quality necessary for the Point's sensible experience is the Intellectual Nature (Thought), the number Eight (*Hod*—Splendor).

NINE: The third quality is the Sense of Being itself. This is the plane of ideation upon which reality depends, the number Nine (*Yesod*—the Foundation).

TEN: Now we have arrived at a fully developed self-consciousness in the physical world, the Zero having expanded itself to Manifestation through these nine successive steps, and therefore become the number Ten (*Malkuth*—the Kingdom), the final Sephira, the concrete existence of the fully manifested Point, the sphere of life on Earth.

THE TWENTY-TWO LETTERS

The Hebrew alphabet is considered to be the vehicle by which God progressively called forth the physical universe through sound, as well as the means of return to the state of divine union. In the *Sepher Yetzirah*, the 22 "foundation" letters are divided into three groups: the three *Mother* letters (corresponding to the elements of Fire, Water, and Air), seven *Double* letters (corresponding to the planets), and 12 *Simple* letters (corresponding to the astrological signs). Detailed meanings and attributions of the Hebrew letters are given in the chapter on Tarot.

The Hebrew language is an alphanumeric language; i.e., the 22 letters do double duty because they also represent numbers. Thus, a word can either be a term or a number. If two words have the same numeric value, the kabbalistic method of exegesis, called *Gematria*, suggests that they have a related esoteric meaning as well. The most common example given to demonstrate the technique of Gematria is the analysis of the word Love, *AHBH*. Its value is 13, the sum of A(1) + H(5) + B(2) + H(5). Another word whose value is 13 is One, or Unity, *AChD*, A(1) + Ch (8) + D(4). One could therefore state, "The nature of Love is Unity." Similarly, the holy and mysterious name of God, *IHVH*, has a value of 26, the sum of I(10) + H(5) + V(6) + H(5). Since 26 is 13 x 2, one could say, "The nature of God is both Love and Unity."

This kind of analysis, however, can lead to paths of speculation that may be considered heretical, unorthodox, or dangerous. By way of illustration, the name of the Serpent who tempted Eve in the Garden is *NChSh*, whose value is 358, N(50) + Ch(8) + Sh(300). Similarly, the word Messiah is *MShICh*, whose value is 358, M(40) + Sh(300) + I(10) + Ch(8). One could therefore state, "The Serpent who tempted Eve in the Garden is the Messiah." This example should help to demonstrate why the study of Kabbalah is reserved in an esoteric manner, so that students may be guided by more experienced and wiser Adepts. It should also help to clarify the position of secrecy within the Mystery Traditions. Information can be dangerous without the proper guidance and direction needed to interpret and comprehend it. All the disciplines discussed in this book have at one time or another been deeply shrouded in secrecy.

The Kabbalah involves many other aspects. These include breathing techniques; yoga-like postures that may resemble certain letter shapes; extensive meditation techniques based on a deeper penetration of the root meanings of the letters; meditations that focus on the Tree of Life, or other diagrams, designed to access deeper layers of consciousness; and magical practices whose purpose is to influence or alter natural events. The following symbols demonstrate some of the richness of that Tradition, as well as the cross-cultural awareness of the Divine Tree as an image of the interaction between Heaven and Earth.

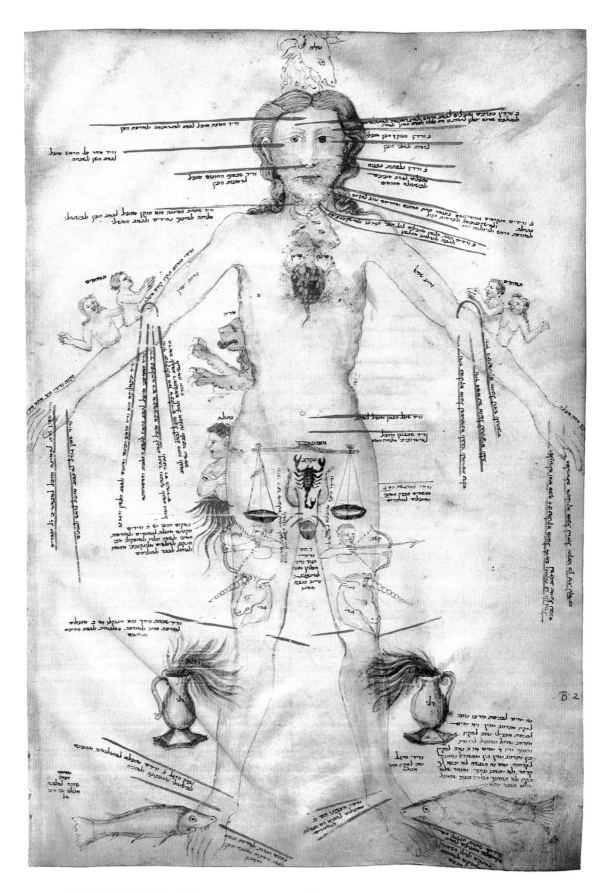

MEDICAL ZODIACAL DIAGRAM (Manuscript illumination, ca. 1400, Italy) The Signs of the Zodiac are shown on the parts of the body they were thought to govern. The red lines indicate where incisions for bleeding could be made. The absence of any specifically Jewish features in the zodiacal glyphs indicates that this figure was copied from a non-Jewish model.

ALCHEMICAL TREE (Manuscript illumination, *Alchemical Treatises* attributed to Raymond Lull) Spanish theologian and mystic Raymond Lull (ca. 1235–1315) traveled throughout western Europe and Moslem lands, preaching and converting the heathen to Christianity. He was a prodigious writer of at least 321 books, an Orientalist who introduced the study of Arabic language into European universities, an eminent early Christian Kabbalist, and, reputedly, an alchemist who had attained the Philosopher's Stone.

THE TREE OF THE SOUL (Illustration, *The Works of Jacob Behmen* [Boehme] by William Law, 1764–1781) The Tree, firmly rooted in the Dark World, extends to the Higher spheres. Passing through the world of Fire, suffering, and experience, it blossoms in the sphere called the Paradise world of greater consciousness, dependent from the sphere of divinity, the Light of Majesty.

LEFT: TREE OF LIFE IN THE FOUR WORLDS (Lithograph by Harry Smith, ca. 1956) This magnificent Tree is published here for the first time. It is based on the Four Worlds of the Kabbalah, each of which is said to contain its own Tree. The *Malkuth* of the higher becomes the *Kether* of the World below. The artist has skillfully layered the Worlds in an intricate original design.

TREE OF THE COSMOS (Illustration by Dionysius Freher, *The Works of Jacob Behmen*) This hand-colored figure expresses the teachings of Boehme (Behmen). The unity of Godhead is depicted in the topmost sphere of Adonai (Lord). The hexagram divides into two triangles, giving birth to the two lower Spheres labeled "Nature" and the "Eternal." They unite in the central explosion labeled *Schrack,* or "The Lightning Flash." The bottom Sphere is the resultant Solar World, in which is depicted the zodiacal band around a central Sun. Compare this with the Solar World sphere of the Boehme design on the facing page.

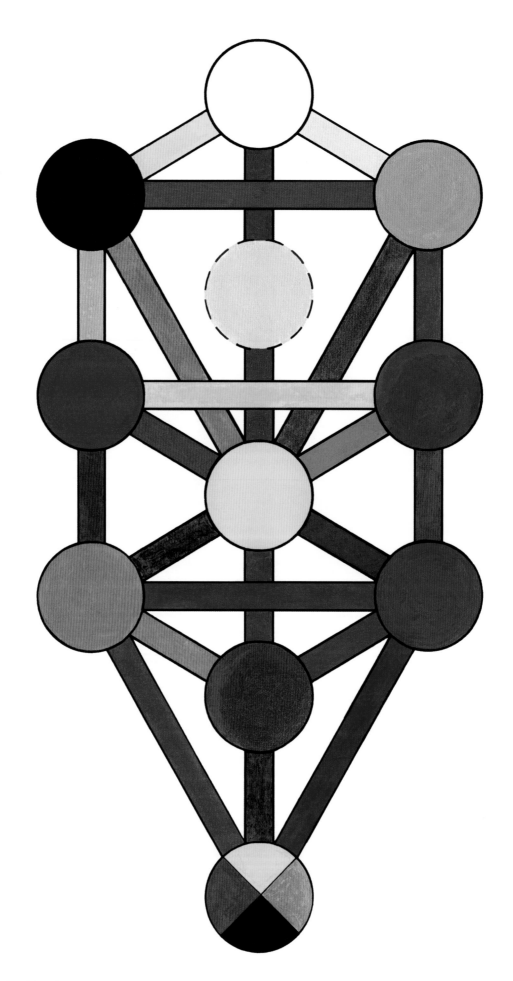

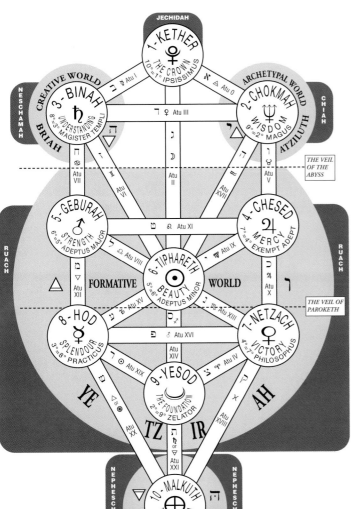

TREE OF LIFE WITH ATTRIBUTIONS
(Computer-generated diagram, designed
by Hymenaeus Beta of Ordo Templi
Orientis, 1992) This Tree gives the traditional
attributions of the Hermetic Kabbalah.
Included are the name, number, Grade of
Initiation, and planet pertaining to the
Sephiroth. The Path attributions include the
Hebrew letter; Tarot card; and Elemental,
Planetary, and Zodiacal correspondences.
Also shown are the Fivefold constitution of
the soul (darker tone) and the Tetragrammaton
in the Four Worlds (lighter tone). This diagram
graphically illustrates the interconnectedness
of esoteric disciplines to one another.

OPPOSITE: **TREE OF LIFE** (Painting by James
and Nancy Wasserman, 1992, revised 1996)
The traditional colors of the Tree of Life in the
Hermetic Kabbalah are derived from the
Golden Dawn. We have included the
"Invisible Sephira," *Daath* (fourth sphere from
the top in gray-white), referred to in the
Kabbalah chapter as the "Abyss between the
Ideal and the Real."

FRATER ACHAD'S COSMIC SNOWFLAKE
(Painted by Steffi Grant, reproduced in *The
Hidden Lore* by Kenneth and Steffi Grant,
1989) Frater Achad was the magical name of
Charles Stansfeld Jones, at one time a devoted
pupil of Aleister Crowley. His geometric and
kabbalistic diagrams and drawings are excellent meditation glyphs. *The Cosmic Snowflake*
was originally drawn for Achad by Will
Ransom and appeared in black and white in
The Anatomy of the Body of God.

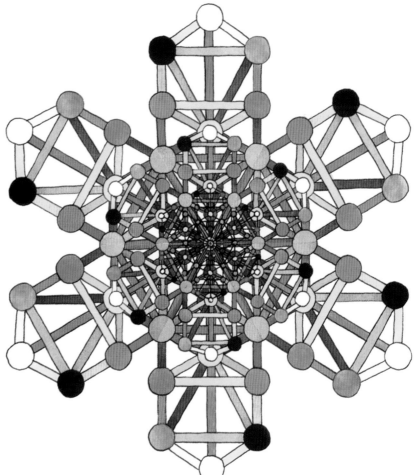

ISIS AND NEPTHYS IN ADORATION OF THE ANKH (*The Papyrus of Ani,* 19th Dynasty, ca. 1250 B.C.E., Egypt) These twin goddesses are the wives and sisters of the brothers, Osiris and Set. The Ankh stands on a Djed pillar—a symbol of stability and duration, in the body representing the spinal column. The Ankh by shape is suggestive of a sandal strap, which implies the power to walk freely, "to go." It may also be taken as an image of sexual intercourse—which implies immortality, the power of the soul "to go."

BUDDHIST ASSEMBLY TREE (Thanka, ca. 17th century, Katmandu, Nepal) This thanka depicts the lineage composed of the various gurus and celestial beings who have been responsible for the teachings of the Dharma (the Buddhist religious doctrine).

BIRTH OF ADONIS (Ceramic bowl by Urbino, 16th century, Northern Italy) The birth of the Greek god of vegetation, Adonis, from the trunk of a myrrh tree after a ten-month gestation was celebrated on December 25th. An early example of the Dying God myth examined at length by Sir James G. Frazer in *The Golden Bough,* his resurrection was celebrated after three days in the tomb, on March 25th. His cult dates to the 7th century B.C.E. in Greece, Babylon, and Syria. His proper name is Tammuz, "true son." Adonis is an appellation meaning "Lord," a title by which he was addressed. The annual death and rebirth of nature was celebrated in myths and rituals throughout the ancient world.

OPPOSITE: THE TREE OF LIFE AND DEATH (Miniature by Berthold Furtmeyer, *Missal of the Archbishop of Salzburg,* 1481) The Tree of Life is pictured with the crucified Christ, and Mary nourishing the righteous with the consecrated host. It is shown as one with the Tree of the Knowledge of Good and Evil, or Death, of which the serpent bade Eve to taste. This aspect of the Tree provides nourishment for the wicked, plucked by the serpent and dispensed by Eve. An angel stands to the left of the Tree of Life, a skeleton to the right of the Tree of Death. It is an unusual image to find within a mainstream Christian context. Good and Evil emanate from the same physical basis and are equally capable of nourishing their adherents. This recalls the Gnostic Manichean doctrine, derived from the earlier Zoroastrians, of the necessity of the conflict between Good and Evil.

MASONIC SEAL OF THE DOUBLE HEADED EAGLE (Illustration by J. A. Knapp, *The Secret Teachings of All Ages* by Manly P. Hall, 1925)

INITIATION

Doubtful are the words, and dark are the ways, but in Thy words and ways is light. Thus then, now as ever, I enter the path of darkness, if haply so I may attain the light. —*Invocation of Horus,* Aleister Crowley[1]

MAN IS SEPARATED FROM HIS DIVINE NATURE by the seemingly impassable barrier of the rational mind and ego. Yet we share an implicit awareness that a higher state exists within us partaking of the nature of the Sacred. We are capable of a deeper communion with a source of power far greater than any we can access by physical strength.

The search for union may well be said to be the root motivation behind human existence. While the basis of this drive is both mysterious and elusive, its power is great, and all intellectual attempts to discredit or deny it pale before its universality.

Iamblichus, the 4th century Neoplatonist known throughout the ancient world as "the Divine Iamblichus," states in *On the Mysteries of the Egyptians, Chaldeans and Assyrians* that, "an innate knowledge of the Gods is coexistent with our very existence; and this knowledge is superior to all judgment and deliberate choice, and subsists prior to reason and demonstration."[2]

Why the chasm exists between us and that with which we seek union is another great mystery. Legends of a Fall exist in many different forms to attempt to explain it. An existential angst, perhaps best described as the fear of nonbeing, permeates the underlayers of our psyches. The Hindu concept of the Day and Night of Brahma may help to explain the roots of this fear. They believe the Universe breathes in and out over vast cycles of time, expanding and contracting so that Creation is periodically annihilated and reborn. Perhaps our basic fear is of the darkness of absorption into the One. The purpose of Initiation, however, is not to explain the Fall or the fear but to bridge the gap between us and our divine origin and birthright.

MYSTERIES IN MAN

The primary "secret" of the Wisdom Tradition is Gnosis: direct experience of the Divine within the human body—no vague promise of grace in an afterlife, but tangible, physical experience of God in the here and now. This is one reason why religion tends to frown on Initiation: The Mysteries defuse the concept of the exclusivity of the Word so often claimed by religion. The individual becomes the Knower.

INVISIBLE GUIDES AND HIGHER INTELLIGENCE

The concept of invisible guides and helpers of humanity is as widespread as the belief that the sun will rise. These guides have been called gods, archangels, angels, saints, mahatmas, inner plane adepts, dhyani buddhas, or ancestors. In legends, ancient civilizations like Atlantis and Lemuria sent forth great teachers to early man to bring the gifts of civilization, such as farming, medicine, and the astronomical secrets of seasonal planting.

Inner Plane Adepts charged with the guidance of humanity, often called the Great White Brotherhood, are perceived as the Intelligences directing the inner workings of occult Orders and individual initiation. The Initiate believes that these higher Intelligences mysteriously and invisibly guide aspirants closer to Themselves. The progressive inner revelations and stimulations of the psychic body are indiscernible by normal perception but are felt in the lives of the candidates who experience genuine Initiation. It is also believed that individuals may contact these Hidden Masters through their own efforts, unaided by formal membership or ritual and ceremony.

Iamblichus states:

The Gods, being benevolent and propitious, impart their light to theurgists in unenvying abundance, calling upwards their souls to themselves, procuring them a union with themselves, and accustoming them, while yet in body, to be separated from bodies, and to be led round to their eternal and intelligible principle. . . . The ascent through invocations imparts to the priests purification from passions, a liberation from generation, and a union with a divine principle. . . . An invocation of this kind does not draw down the impassive and pure Gods to that which is passive and impure; but, on the contrary, it renders us . . . pure and immutable.[3]

CHARACTER DEVELOPMENT

Development of character is absolutely essential for Initiation. The moral teachings contained within *The Golden Verses of Pythagoras* are an excellent source of guidance on this subject. A similar teaching is expressed in the beautiful precepts of the 11th century Sufi Master, Sheikh Abdullah Ansari:

The law of life requires
1. Sincerity to God.
2. Severity to self.
3. Justice to all people.
4. Service to elders.
5. Kindness to the young.
6. Generosity to the poor.
7. Good counsel to friends.
8. Forbearance with enemies.
9. Indifference to fools.
10. Respect to the learned.[4]

Aleister Crowley expresses the same principles in more contemporary language:

The fact of a person being a gentleman is as much an ineluctable factor as any possible spiritual experience; in fact, it is possible, even probable, that a man may be misled by the enthusiasm of an illumination, and if he should find apparent conflict between his spiritual duty and his duty to honour, it is almost sure evidence that a trap is being laid for him and he should unhesitatingly stick to the course which ordinary decency indicates.[5]

Iamblichus advances prayer as one of the best techniques of character development.

No operation, however, in sacred concerns, can succeed without the intervention of prayer . . . the divine key, which opens to men the penetralia of the Gods, accustoms us to the splendid rivers of supernal light, in a short time perfects our inmost recesses and disposes them for the ineffable embrace and contact of the Gods; and does not desist till it raises us to the summit of all.[6]

To interact fully with our intrinsic Luminous Divinity, it is necessary to open the heart to the True Self. We must annihilate the false, error-ridden self of our daily affairs. John Donne expresses his yearning for the liberation of annihilation in startlingly violent but eloquent terms. He dramatically describes the stubborn and rebellious nature of the ego, the enemy of the Light of the Mysteries.

Batter my heart, three-personed God; for, you
As yet but knock, breathe, shine, and seek to mend;

That I may rise, and stand, o'erthrow me, and bend
Your force, to break, blow, burn, and make me new.
. . .
Yet dearly I love you, and would be loved fain,
But I am betrothed unto your enemy,
Divorce me, untie, or break that knot again,
Take me to you, imprison me, for I
Except you enthral me, shall never be free,
Nor ever chaste, except you ravish me.[7]

Initiation is complex and demands a disciplined psychological equilibrium. One must learn to find the balance between divine illumination and everyday reality. The progressive nature of initiation allows one to sustain the luminous experience for longer periods of time, thereby integrating it more fully into daily life. However, the ecstasy of divine ravishment may lead to a "confusing of the planes." A modern urban aphorism states that the successful invocation of the Lord of the Universe—and a token—will get you on a subway. It cannot be too highly emphasized that the mystic swims in the same waters in which the psychotic drowns. Equilibrium is the basis of the Work.

THE QUEST AND THE SPIRITUAL BATTLE

A common thread linking the initiatic experience in various Mystery Traditions is a descent of some kind into a dark and fearful underworld. Here the only protection is strength of faith—commitment to duty and a higher purpose whose agency will protect the candidate through the deadly trials that lie ahead. These trials often take the shape of battles with overwhelmingly strong and violent chthonic enemies in the form of dragons, giants, serpents, and the like. To prevail, the Initiate will battle to near exhaustion. He is then granted some form of reward, such as secret knowledge, the king's daughter, wealth, or eternal life.

In the land of the trial, the candidate is likely to meet helpers or guides who bring him wisdom. These may be in the form of animals who speak and direct him to the next stages, shades of loved ones in the realm of the dead who instruct him, or genies and spirits who provide missing keys to various riddles.

The final reward is the knowledge of the inner strength that the candidate was challenged to call forth within himself, including the now-tested awareness that the intuitive certainty of his mission was a true inspiration. This belief exposed him to death and much suffering, yet his survival and triumph have confirmed the necessity of the journey. The power of this conviction

lasts a lifetime. The "real secrets" of Initiation are incommunicable because they are internal.

WESTERN SECRET SOCIETIES

The historical lineage of Initiation in Western culture begins in the temples of Egypt. From Egypt, the Mysteries moved to Greece: for Pythagoras and other early masters of philosophy traveled to Egypt to converse with her priests and Initiates. Greek adepts celebrated a mythological panorama of Olympian deities and animated nature spirits and promoted their teaching through the Eleusinian Mysteries.

The Gnostics represent the next development. Essene communities in the Holy Land and other pre-Christian, Jewish, and Pagan Gnostics initially welcomed the Christian revelation, finding in its teachings a familiar echo of their own ideas. Christian Gnostics became part of the rich religious tapestry of the area, which was also influenced by the growth of the Mithraic religion throughout the Roman Empire. The Neoplatonists were the first to protest the exclusivity and increasing militancy of Christianity. Intolerance of other beliefs was introduced largely by St. Paul and grew progressively worse as Christianity assumed greater political power in the Roman Empire. Constantine declared it the state religion in 325. In 415, an enraged mob of Christian monks murdered Hypatia, famed leader of the Alexandrian Neoplatonic school—sounding the death knell for philosophic tolerance and driving the Mysteries underground for nearly six centuries.

When Justinian closed the Neoplatonic academies in the Roman Empire in 529, pagan scholars and mystics were forced to flee. They were welcomed in Persia. The Gnostic teachings flourished in the East, in anticipation of their next major migration, which would take place during the Crusades.

In 1095, Pope Urban II was able to launch the First Crusade. The Holy Land contained the seeds of the later Renaissance. Arab culture was at its highest and most refined. European Christianity was now added to the area's religious landscape. The mystics, fakirs, Zoroastrians, Gnostics, Sufis, and Buddhists must have presented a kaleidoscopic panorama to the newly arrived Crusaders. Increasing doubt of the exclusive possession of divine favor by Christianity would gradually undermine the orthodoxy of some. The Knights Templar and other military orders remained in the Holy Land during the two centuries of Western occupation. Generations were born and raised in a culture entirely alien to that of their European ancestors.

The Templars were more than once accused of collusion with the Assassins, or Hashishim, a Shiite Islamic group in modern Iraq founded in 1090 by Hasan-i-Sabah. There are legitimate historical records of necessary political interaction between the two groups. The Assassins were a hierarchically organized mystical Order and secret society, credited with being the structural model for many later esoteric societies. They are believed to have been a major influence in the spread of Sufism within Islam. It is widely accepted that they shared their knowledge with individual Templar knights who carried that Wisdom back to Europe.

The first literature of the Grail tradition appeared nearly simultaneously with the founding of the Knights Templar in the 11th century. Wolfram von Eschenbach's *Parzival*,[8] a Grail Romance of the late 12th century, includes many Templar figures. Pauline Matarasso's *Quest of the Holy Grail*[9] identifies the monks who guided the Grail Knights as Cistercians on the basis of their white robes, their isolation as hermits, and the doctrines they taught to the Grail Companions. St. Bernard of Clairvaux, who wrote the Rule for the Knights Templar, was an important member of the Cistercian Order. He was also the Templar champion with the pope and the wealthy nobility in the early years of the Order's dramatic rise to power.

After the Crusades ended in defeat, the Templars themselves were destroyed throughout Europe under orders of King Phillip IV and Pope Clement V. All known members of the Order in France were arrested in a single night in 1307, accused of heretical doctrines and practices; the truth of these accusations is still the subject of scholarly debate. While thousands died, some European kings merely paid lip service to the pope's orders to arrest, torture, and kill the Templars residing in their countries. Surviving Order members went quietly underground and shared their doctrines with hand-picked disciples.

The Tarot, introduced in the 14th century, is replete with Grail and Templar symbolism. The Renaissance Neoplatonic Hermetic revival (discussed in the chapter on Magick) began during the 15th century. In the 16th and 17th Centuries, Alchemy and Rosicrucianism came to simultaneous prominence; both included a secret doctrine whose progressive unfoldment was the primary teaching method. Masonry—which still preserves a Knights Templar Degree—achieved widespread prominence in the 18th century. Mozart's *Magic Flute* is a beautiful rendition of the Rosicrucian/Masonic myth. A political agenda was ascribed to Masonry by many, and in fact, it is still rumored that the destruction of the monarchy in the French Revolution was Masonic vengeance for the crushing of the Templars in 1307.

The 19th century saw a flowering of occult societies. P. B. Randolph's Hermetic Brotherhood of Light was highly influential in continental esoteric circles. The Theosophical Society, founded by Madame Blavatsky in 1875, was responsible for a major infusion of the Mystery Teachings in the West. The Golden Dawn, founded in England in 1888, included prominent poets, writers, and people involved in theater, who spread the word through the arts. The Ordo Templi Orientis, founded in Germany in 1895, began active propagation in the English-speaking world in 1912 when Aleister Crowley became its English leader.

Esoteric societies founded in the 20th century include the Stella Matutina, an offshoot of the Golden Dawn. Among its members were such luminaries as Dion Fortune and Israel Regardie. The Builders of the Adytum, founded by Paul Foster Case, patterns its teachings on the Tarot. Other modern groups include Rosicrucian fellowships, Pagan and Wiccan groups of mixed traditions, and followers of the teachings of G. I. Gurdjieff and Rudolf Steiner. Smaller groups also exist, gathered around individual teachers and studying specific disciplines such as Alchemy, Pythagorean philosophy, and other areas of occult research. In addition, there are groups placing less emphasis on hierarchy and secrecy and structured along broader philosophical interests, such as the Philosophical Research Society.

Our illustrations represent various stages of the initiatic experience, beginning with images of traditional esoteric physiology. These are followed by examples of Initiation in the ancient and medieval worlds, including the Grail Mysteries and their unique blending of Christianity and Paganism. Finally, we present images of the Spiritual Battle, a section of Renaissance Rosicrucian symbols, and examples of the iconography of modern secret societies.

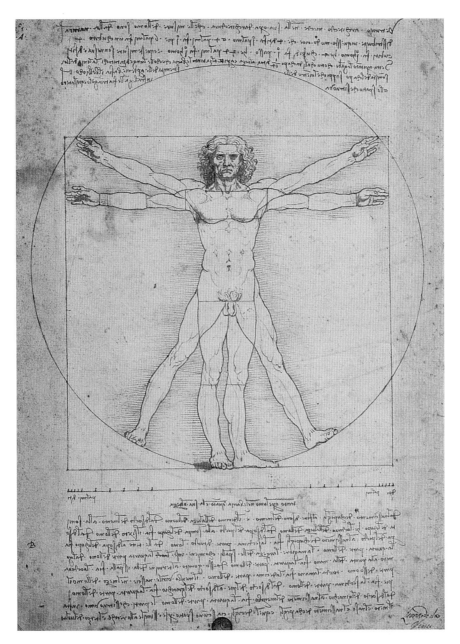

THE PROPORTIONS OF THE HUMAN FIGURE ACCORDING TO VITRUVIUS
(Drawing by Leonardo da Vinci, ca. 1510) The geometry of the human body is
indicative of the highest mysteries of the cosmos. The circle may be formed from a
person lying on his back, with a compass placed at the navel. The square is formed
from the measure of the height from head to toe, and the width of the outstretched
arms. Man is a microcosm, the perfect image of the universe.

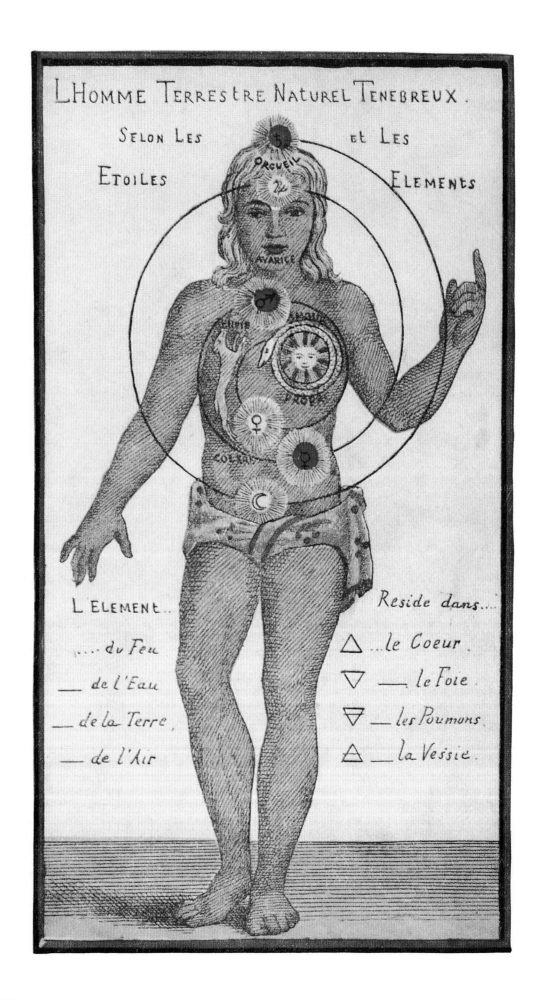

EGYPTIAN TEMPLE (Drawing by artists of the Napoleonic Expedition, ca. 1799) The conquest of Egypt by France involved some 34,000 soldiers, sailors, and marines, accompanied by about 500 civilians, including approximately 150 architects, artists, students, scientists, and engineers, who faithfully recorded the monuments that overwhelmed them with their ancient splendor. This temple from the Isle of Philae is a beautiful reminder of the grandeur of the Egyptian religious culture. The Napoleonic expedition left a powerful artistic account of Egypt before the damage that would occur during the next 200 years. The Rosetta Stone, which later revealed the keys to the Egyptian hieroglyphic language, was discovered during this same expedition.

OPPOSITE: CHAKRAS (Painting by Johann Georg Gichtel, reproduced in *Theosophica Practica* by William Law, 1898) A 17th century pupil of Boehme, Gichtel called this diagram "the Condition of Man in his old, lapsed, and corrupted State; without any respect to or consideration of his renewing by Regeneration." William Law further describes the state as being "after his Fall in Pollution and Perdition. . . . " The labels on the figure read *Pride, Avarice, Envy, Love, Possessiveness, Anger.* This is the entirely earthly, natural man prior to Initiation.

PSYCHOSTASIA (Drawing by Lucy Lamy, from the Temple of Der-el-Medinet) The Weighing of the Heart scene from the Book of the Dead shows the deceased, or candidate, standing between Maat of the Two Horizons. His heart is on the balance, weighed against Maat's Feather of Truth. The scales balance. Thoth records this and announces the presence of the candidate to Osiris, before whom stand the Sons of Horus, and the Ammenit beast who would have devoured the candidate had his sins weighed down the balance. The candidate himself is in the posture of Hoor-paar-Kraat, the child god and Lord of Silence. The innocence of the now "justified" deceased is thus represented.

CONSECRATION BY HORUS AND SET OF SETI I (Tracing of papyrus, Thebes, 19th Dynasty, in *The Gods of the Egyptians* by E. A. Wallis-Budge, 1904) The deities are showering the pharaoh, Seti I, with Ankhs poured forth from the vases held in their hands. The Ankh is a symbol of life, fertility, and immortality. (See caption page 30.)

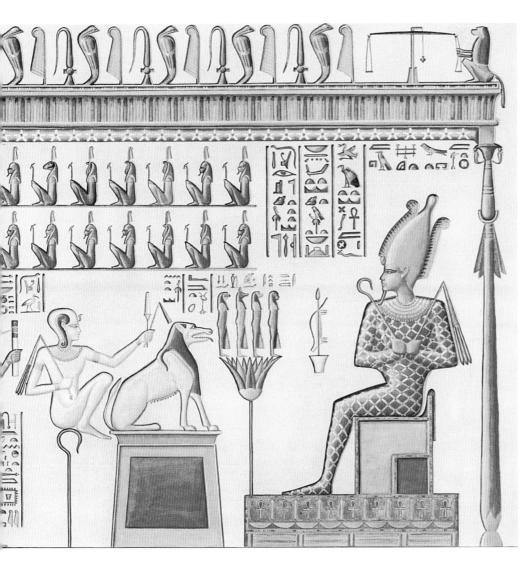

PROPHECY (Engraving by Johann de Bry, *Tomi Secundi Tractatus . . .* by Robert Fludd, 1620)
This scene may represent Elijah anointing Elisha or perhaps Samuel anointing David. The horn of oil and the Spirit in the shape of a dove, issuing from above, represent the influx of divine grace on the candidate through the mentor, or Initiator, who acts as a vehicle of the cosmic force. Compare this with the ancient Egyptian representation on the facing page.

PYTHAGORAS (Illustration, *The History of Philosophy* by Thomas Stanley, 1655–1662, hand-colored by Jim Harter) The father of Western Philosophy and Initiation, Pythagoras passed on his teachings orally; they are known to us only through his disciples. The moral laws taught in his Academy included a five-year probation of silence and meditation, temperance, vegetarianism, and secrecy regarding the teachings. *The Golden Verses* are the most important surviving fragments of his teachings.

OPPOSITE ABOVE: **TRIPOTOLEMUS BETWEEN DEMETER AND KORE (Roman replica of Greek bas-relief from the 5th century B.C.E.)** Kore was abducted by Hades while she was gathering flowers in a field. In protest of Zeus's approval of the abduction, her mother, Demeter, Goddess of Corn, left Olympus and wandered on earth, disguised as an old woman. She arrived at Eleusis, ruled by the wise King Celeus, whose kindness induced her to stay and nurse Celeus's newborn son. The king's eldest son, Tripotolemus, was the first initiate in Demeter's Eleusian mysteries and spread the benefit of agriculture throughout Greece.

OPPOSITE BELOW: **INANNA (Mesopotamian Cylinder Seal, 3rd millennium B.C.E.)** The descent of Inanna, or Ishtar, is the oldest myth of the journey of death and rebirth. Inanna was the Sumerian Queen of Heaven, who decided to visit her sister, Ereshkigal, Queen of the Underworld. At each of the seven gates of the underworld she was ordered to remove one of her symbols of power. Naked, she was murdered by Ereshkigal. After three days she was revived and reborn. She is depicted with a female worshiper or minor goddess raising her hand in a gesture of adoration.

ABOVE: **VISION OF THE HOLY GRAIL** (Tapestry by William Morris to the design of Burne Jones, ca. 1890) The Grail was said to be the cup that caught the blood Jesus shed during the crucifixion. It may also have been the cup that he used to celebrate the Passover at the Last Supper. The various versions of the Grail myth derive from the fact that it was an oral tradition, whose individual tellers would embellish and change the story at will. The Horn of Plenty, the Cauldron of Immortality, and the Ever-full Vessel are Pagan antecedents of the Grail. The Grail is variously described as a cup of intensely beautiful light, a plate from which each person received the meal of his choice or the consecrated host, or a stone with the power to heal and bring plenitude. In this beautiful image, Galahad kneels at the door of the chapel while the knights, Bors and Percival, who were less spiritually pure, remain some distance away. The Lance, held by the angel with the plate, is that which pierced the side of Jesus as he hung upon the cross.

OPPOSITE BOTTOM: **ESTOIRE GIVEN TO HERMIT** (Manuscript illumination, *Estoire del Saint Graal,* 15th century, France) Joseph of Arimathaea is said to have brought the Grail to Britain. Joseph either collected the blood at the site or received the cup in a vision. Tradition has it that the authors of the *Estoire del Saint Graal* received their story from a heavenly source. Here the Dove of the Holy Spirit descends with the book in which the story is written, while God the Father and God the Son watch from above.

RIGHT: **SIR GALAHAD** (Manuscript illumination, ca. 1290, France) Galahad was introduced into the Grail Romance cycle somewhat later in the *Quest of the Holy Grail* (1215–1230). The communion host is of course the sacred image of Christ's body, taught as the Mystery of the Mass during the Last Supper. This was a continuation of the age-old eucharist ceremony. The sacrificial victim changed over time from human, to animal, to consecrated food. Our dependence upon the Divine for nourishment is self-evident, both in science and in myth.

THE TEMPTATION OF ST. ANTHONY (Painting by Hieronymus Bosch, ca. 1510) St. Anthony sits in meditation with his companion pig. A sinister, menacing terror becomes the means for tempting the Saint. A creature emerges from the pond; others bring a jug of alcohol; demons and the Boschian hybrids amass to disgust Anthony and torment the pig.

ST. GEORGE AND THE DRAGON (Painting by Raphael, 1505) The image of the dragon slayer celebrates the triumph of virtue over a powerful, instinctual enemy. Its roots go back to Sumer, where the sun god Ninurta slew the dragon Zu. In Egypt, the serpent Apep, or Apophis, was engaged in fierce battle with the sun god Ra each night. The Christian hero St. George recalls the story of Perseus and Andromeda. George was born in Turkey. During his stay in Libya, he learned of a dragon who lived in a pond near the town of Silene. The dragon exhaled poisonous fumes, killing people whenever it approached the walls of the city. To pacify the dragon the inhabitants brought two sheep every day until there were no more sheep. The dragon then killed many more people. The townsfolk decided to bring it a human and a beast each day, consequently suffering the loss of many of their children. The lot fell eventually upon the daughter of the king. On her way to the pond, she met George, who asked the cause of her sorrow. He slew the monster through the power of his belief in Jesus Christ and converted the town to Christianity, baptizing some 20,000 men in addition to women and children. George was adopted as the patron saint of Britain in 1349.

THE MOUNTAIN OF THE PHILOSOPHERS
(Illustration, *The Secret Symbols of the Rosicrucians of the 16th and 17th Centuries*, edited by J. D. A. Eckhard, 1785) This is the sacred Mountain of Initiation or Abiegnus (*Abi Agnus* or Lamb of the Father). Christian Rosenkreutz is seated before the tomb wherein he lay for 120 years, surrounded by various alchemical symbols that hide "the highest treasure in this world." The date of 1604 is that of the opening of his tomb, according to the *Fame and Confession of the Fraternity of the Rosie Cross,* the first Rosicrucian document, published in 1614. The text below the image reads, in part, "Be diligent, peaceful, constant and pious, pray that God may help thee. And if thou attain, never forget the poor. Then thou wilt praise God with the legion of the angels now and forever."

THE COLLEGE OF THE ROSICRUCIAN FRATERNITY (Illustration, *Speculum Sophicum Rhodo-Stauroticum* by Theophilus Schweighardt, 1618) In the upper left, near the man encircled by the crowned serpent, can be seen the date 1604. A Rose and a Cross are inscribed on each side of the doorway. The whole is attached to the hand of the Lord. The trumpet, sword, winged bell tower, shields inscribed with the divine name *IHVH*, scholar studying a globe, and numerous other symbols all point to the doctrines within the sacred college. The philosopher in the lower right is shown "anchored" in a prayer that ascends directly to the Highest.

THE POLISH RIDER (Painting by Rembrandt, 1655) A tradition states that this is a portrait of the mysterious Rosicrucian adept the Comte de Saint Germain, believed to have been an incarnation of Christian Rosenkreutz. *The Comte de Gabalis,* by the Abbe de Villars, "a curious Rosicrucian book," first published in 1670, describes him as, "A Nobleman of high rank and a great Cabalist, whose lands lie towards the frontiers of Poland." The Comte de Saint Germain was the inspiration for the character Zanoni, in the brilliant novel by the same name by Sir Edward Bulwer Lytton, quoted in the Secret Societies chapter.

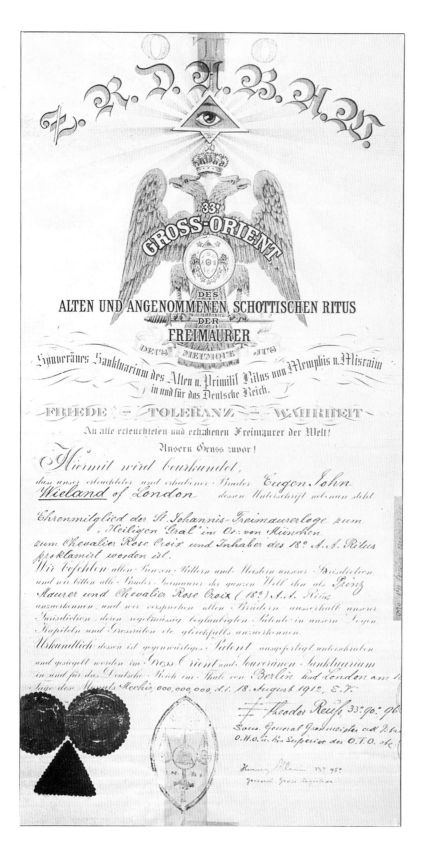

MASONIC CHARTER (1912) Theodor Reuss was an early cofounder of the Ordo Templi Orientis (O.T.O.) with Karl Kellner and Heinrich Klein in 1895. After Kellner's death, Reuss became the Frater Superior, or Outer Head of the Order. He initiated Aleister Crowley in 1912 and appointed him as sovereign head of all English-speaking Order activities. In 1922, Reuss appointed Crowley to succeed him as Frater Superior of the worldwide O.T.O.

OPPOSITE: GOLDEN DAWN CROSS (Painting by Steffi Grant, reproduced in *The Hidden Lore* by Kenneth and Steffi Grant, 1989) This design is the central motif of the Hermetic Order of the Golden Dawn. The Rose Cross within the center is surrounded by the three Mother Letters, seven Double Letters, and twelve Simple Letters of the Hebrew alphabet, as discussed in the Kabbalah chapter. The rays coming off the central rose represent the Word of the Adeptus Minor ritual (see pages 80–82). The symbols of Sulphur, Salt, and Mercury, discussed in the Alchemy chapter, change position around the arms of the cross. The pentagrams are surrounded by the symbols of the four elements plus the fifth element of spirit. The planetary hexagram in the middle is surrounded by the six holy planets with the Sun in the center. The color scheme of the arms of the Cross is linked to the Elemental attributions.

EQUINOX EMBLEM (*The Equinox*, vol. I, by Aleister Crowley, ten issues published between 1909 and 1914) *The Equinox* is the official organ of the A∴A∴, a magical Order founded by Aleister Crowley and George Cecil Jones in 1907 after the breakdown of the Hermetic Order of the Golden Dawn. The A∴A∴ is committed to the teaching of spiritual development and offers a disciplined and multifaceted curriculum for that purpose.

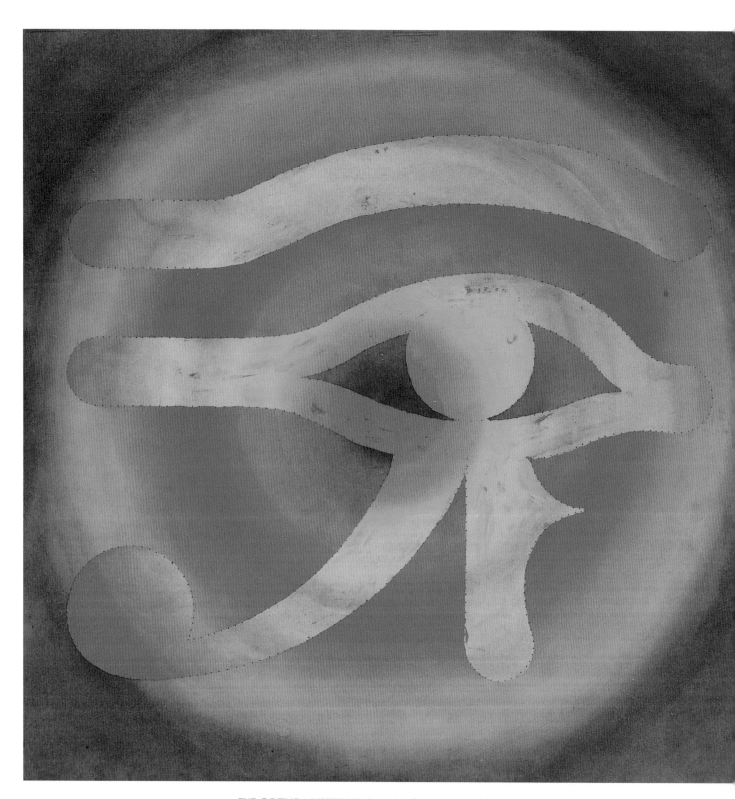

EYE OF THE MYSTERIES (Painting by Harry Smith, ca. 1962)

MAGICK AND THE GODS

... unless you make yourself equal to God, you cannot understand God: for the like is not intelligible save to the like. Make yourself grow to a greatness beyond measure, by a bound free yourself from the body; raise yourself above all time, become Eternity; then you will understand God. Believe that nothing is impossible for you, think yourself immortal and capable of understanding all, all arts, all sciences, the nature of every living being. Mount higher than the highest height; descend lower than the lowest depth. Draw into yourself all sensations of everything created, fire and water, dry and moist, imagining that you are everywhere, on earth, in the sea, in the sky, that you are not yet born, in the maternal womb, adolescent, old, dead, beyond death. If you embrace in your thought all things at once, times, places, substances, qualities, quantities, you may understand God.   —The Mind to Hermes, Hermes Trismegistus[1]

ALEISTER CROWLEY DEFINES MAGICK AS "the science and art of causing change to occur at will."[2] The gods most associated with Magick are the lawgivers, scientists, teachers of writing; weighers and measurers, those who distinguish; gods of proportion, speech, the word, the spell. "In the beginning was the word and the word was with God and the word was God."[3] The Messiah is the Word made flesh, the Logos, sustaining all creation by sound, the *Nam* or *Shabd* of the Sikh mystics, the primordial *AUM* whose vibratory motions are physical reality.

This is the original cosmic "Magical Spell," whose sonorous intonation resulted in the creation of the universe, and upon whose steady waves of sustained will all of life depends. Magick is simply the most basic of universal laws; "Every intentional act is a magical act."[4]

The most familiar magical ceremony today is undoubtedly the transubstantiation of wine and bread performed by the Catholic Church, an act of Magick that is celebrated on a daily basis throughout the Western world. Candle lighting for the dead and all ceremonial actions geared to commemorating or gaining the favor of higher beings—from ancestors, saints, and angels to God

Himself—are based on the magical tradition. Even the prayers said at a presidential inauguration mimic the Egyptian tradition of the semidivine pharaoh guiding society by means of divine direction.

The earliest home of a systematic magical tradition was Egypt. Egyptian religion was a magical religion in the sense that there was a continuous interaction between the individual and the various deities that constituted its pantheon. Formulas and spells were memorized; tests of courage and honor were administered; secret knowledge, along with a highly developed moral character, were required to penetrate into deeper levels of divine consciousness.

Magick played a large part in Greek and later Roman philosophical life, particularly among those pagans unsatisfied with the Christian revelation. The Gnostic thinkers and philosophers who developed the Hermetic literature in the 2nd and 3rd centuries were especially enamored of the Egyptians; often seekers would spend the night in the vicinity of an Egyptian temple in the hope of receiving insights into divine mysteries through dreams. There was also a good deal of contact with oriental philosophies in the religiously tolerant atmosphere of the Roman Empire.

The influence of these nearly forgotten Gnostic thinkers blossomed in 15th century Europe. In 1460, a Greek Gnostic manuscript, containing the primary writings of the Corpus Hermeticum (or body of Hermetic literature), was purchased by the wealthy ruler of Florence, Cosimo de Medici. He was the founder of the Platonic Academy, dedicated to the study of Greek Philosophy, that functioned as a center of Neoplatonic thought. He employed Marselio Ficino, director of the academy, to translate the manuscript, instructing him to immediately abandon his translation of Plato until he could complete the Hermetic writings.

The availability of the Hermetic literature engendered the Renaissance fascination with Magick. A disciple of Ficino's, Pico della Mirandola was the first Christian Adept to introduce the Hebrew Kabbalah into the practice of Renaissance Magick, thus giving birth to the Hermetic Kabbalah.

The ban on Magick by the medieval Church had forced its practitioners to remain concealed, Magick remaining a socially undesirable pursuit. However, the Hermetic writings added an air of respectability and philosophical prestige to the practice of Magick for the first time in the post-Christian West. Magick was a prime component of the Rosicrucian movement, which flourished first in Germany and then throughout Europe in the 16th and 17th centuries. This continued in the 18th century, as the mysterious Comte de St. Germaine, Cagliostro, and others taught Magick throughout the growing number of continental Masonic Lodges. In the 19th century, through the writings of Éliphas Lévi in France, and the later workings of the Hermetic Order of the Golden Dawn in Britain, Magick burst full-view into the intellectual life of the Western world. Finally, in the 20th century, a brilliant synthesis of Magick was provided by the controversial English Adept, Aleister Crowley; and today, Magick has become virtually a household word thanks in no small degree to the efforts of J. K. Rowling and her young Magus Harry Potter.

Magick is one of the most basic of human tendencies. It ranges in the popular imagination from the level of infantile wish-fulfillment of common desires to the superstitious and neurotic fixations of magical thinking: "Step on a crack and break your mother's back." In some cases magical thinking can be carried straight through to psychosis; it is in fact a hallmark of psychotic symptoms.

Magick is the least commonly understood of the subjects treated in this book. The blind that is presented by Magick is the gratification of the ego—in much the same way that the blind presented by Alchemy is the acquisition of material wealth. The ego by nature is engaged in continual grasping for the fulfillment of its limitless demands. Anything that seems to offer the desired end will be seized with talons of determination. People who are promised victory over enemies, triumph over poverty, or fulfillment of romantic dreams—and who cannot see beyond these temptations—will search fruitlessly for the nonexistent and give up. Those who persist will be led by the work itself to reject lesser rewards and achieve the results that are possible. Milarepa, the great Saint and Sage of the Nyingma lineage of Tibetan Buddhism, originally entered the Magical Path to perform "black" Magick. He was transformed by the required work into one of the greatest religious teachers of all time.

The *siddhis*, or powers unleashed by assiduous practices, are a goal for some, a hindrance to others, and a simple reality to those whose life purpose is the fulfillment of Divine Law. This is not to say that "black" Magick does not work. However, it functions only in the lowest realm and often requires more energy than is necessary when one can make use of ordinary channels. An old magical aphorism points out that it may be easier and more convenient to take a boat than to attempt walking on water.

What is the other side of Magick that has been referred to by the author of the *Goetia* as "the Highest, most Absolute, and most Divine Knowledge of Natural Philosophy"?[5]

Magick can be said to be the expansion of human consciousness through the willed interaction with greater levels of consciousness than we possess ourselves or of which we are usually aware in normal life. Whether gods or spirits exist "out there" or within ourselves is not the issue. The question is, how can we contact Them and thereby raise our level of consciousness to a more advanced state?

The Magician's attunement to the all-sustaining and underlying current of universal energy requires a pure and ordered life. The body must be fully mastered so that it will not distract the Magus in his or her conjuration. The active, chattering monkey-mind must be capable of supreme quiet and unwavering concentration on a single idea, unaffected by outside interference.

On the intellectual plane, the symbol set employed by the Magician must be capable of suggesting to his taut mental state the one idea with which he is working, again and again through all the senses. The laws of analogy and the theory of correspondence ascribe colors, herbs, perfumes, geometrical patterns, oils, and other symbols to various archetypes—planets, gods, Sephiroth on the Tree of Life, and so forth.

The Magician will first ascertain through meditation, possibly combined with divination, what idea he or she needs to emphasize in the individual psyche. Having determined a goal, the Magician will study the symbolic attributions of that idea.

An invocation will be developed that calls upon the mythical aspects of the energy invoked. If that energy is a god, the attributes of the deity will be listed and personally embraced as if they were the Magician's own, as the psycho-spiritual process of progressive identification with the higher state of mind develops. The invocation will be written and memorized over the course of weeks or months. Our Magus will likely visit a library to search for traditional images of the god and will learn to paint them, both by copying and from memory.

Using the theory of correspondence as a further basis for action, the Magus will determine an appropriate astrological timing for the rite. If a mercurial energy is being invoked, for example, Wednesday may be chosen, as it is the day that corresponds to Mercury. If the importance of the invocation dictates, it may be timed to occur in Gemini or Virgo, both ruled by Mercury, and further timed to coincide with an exact moment during which the planet is in particularly good astrological aspect, as determined through the use of an ephemeris.

An appropriately colored robe will be worn, possibly handmade for this specific rite. A Circle will be constructed that will include a numbered set of candles of appropriate color, arranged in the proper geometric pattern to further suggest the idea. The list goes on: incense is chosen, an appropriate series of knocks is struck on the Bell, and so forth, all to repeatedly suggest the one idea to as many of the senses as possible.

Magick may be understood as an active Western form of Yoga. Its purpose is the progressive union with an increasingly sophisticated series of ideas leading to the ultimate invocation of, and union with, God. Its particular appeal to the Western mind lies in its emphasis on uniting rational intellect with mystical aspiration. Of course, the intellect must be abandoned as the rite builds to a crescendo, but it is indispensable in the preparatory stages.

The reader who is unfamiliar with Magick must understand that the process described here is not brief. One invocation may take as long as a year to perform. Magick is not, as so many have misunderstood it to be, a lazy man's way of overcoming universal laws, or of cheating his way through the trials of life!

In a review of a modern magical grimoire (ceremonial spellbook), William Burroughs wrote, "Is there not something skulking and cowardly about this Adept, hiding in his magic circle and forcing demons to do the dirty jobs he is afraid to do himself, like some Mafia don behind his bulletproof glass giving orders to his hit men?"[6] This is clearly not the type of Magick described in this book. There is a darker side to Magick, but many have found that the consequences of abusing occult energies will rebound negatively on anyone who undertakes the abuse. We focus here on the Magick of Light and Life.

In the images that follow, we begin by looking at the archetypal gods and goddesses most closely identified with Magick. We then trace the image of the Magician through various artists and present symbols of operative magical iconography. Finally, those teachers deemed most influential in the modern magical tradition of the last century are presented. Other excellent works of magical literature may be found in the reading list.

THOTH (*Papyrus of Hunefer*, 19th dynasty, ca. 1310 B.C.E., Egypt) God of Magick, Writing, Measurement, and Science, Thoth, or Tahuti, is the progenitor of the Word Gods. Several others from other cultures are shown on this spread, all of whom share the same basic function in their respective pantheons. Other incarnations of the Word God archetype, not shown here, include Ganesha among the Hindus, Eleggua in the African-Voudon tradition, and Mercury in Roman myth.

ODIN (Statue by Hermann Ernst Freund, early 19th century) Founder of the Mysteries of Scandinavia, Odin is the God of Magick and the runes (the Norse magical alphabet). His gifts include poetry, learning, and the rules of society. He is also the war god, although he fights with magical powers. He is the Ruler of the Underworld and the Psychopomp (the guide of souls through the realm of the Dead). The two ravens (representing thought and memory) fly around the world daily to bring him news, and the two wolves (the past and the future) relate to his function as guide of the dead. Odin voluntarily sacrificed one of his eyes to drink from the fountain of wisdom at the roots of the world tree Yggdrasil. He hung upside down from that Tree for nine days and nights, after which he was given the gift of the runes and experienced physical regeneration in this variation of the crucifixion myth.

ΘΕΟC

HERMES (Illustration, *De Divinatione et magicis praestigiis* by Jean Jacques Boissard, ca. 1615) Hermes, the Greek derivative of Thoth, is also known as the wing-footed Messenger of the Gods, the God of Thieves, and the trickster. In his aspect of "Thrice-Greatest," or "Trismegistus," Hermes is closer to the majestic and intellectual Thoth. The Hermetic writings were compiled by different individuals all using the same pseudonym.

MANJUSRI (Painting, 18th century, Nepal) Manjusri is the Wisdom deity in the Tibetan Buddhist pantheon. He is always shown with the sword, which denotes the intellectual, analytical facility. His other primary attribute, the Book of Wisdom, is most often depicted enveloped by flowers and floating near his shoulder. It is attached to a cord held close to his heart, indicating that the basis of the living wisdom is love. This rare image of Manjusri depicts him in union with his consort.

THE DUAL GOD, HORUS-SET (Tracing of papyrus in *The Gods of the Egyptians* by E. A. Wallis-Budge, 1904) Set, the jackal-headed deity, one of the oldest gods of the Egyptian pantheon, was often considered the "devil." He was the slayer of Osiris and at times the deadly enemy of Horus. Horus is the hawk-headed Lord, the Face of Heaven whose eyes were the Sun and the Moon. Horus is Lord of the North and the sky by day; Set is Lord of the South and the sky by night. They personify Good and Evil, Life and Death, and all other forms of duality. They are depicted in this very old and unusual figure as a complementary unity.

ABRAXAS (Design from 2nd century Gnostic gem, reproduced in *The Gnostics and Their Remains* by C. W. King, 1887) Abraxas is the Gnostic deity whose name, in the Greek Kabbalah, equates to 365—the number of days in the year. Hence he is a solar deity. His rooster's head also confirms this attribution. Abraxas is a god who combines good and evil in a unity. The serpents that form his legs imply a sexual aspect.

BAPHOMET (Illustration, *Transcendental Magic* by Éliphas Lévi, 1896) This multilevel symbol represents the mysterious God of the Templars, the fearsome androgyne with a woman's breasts and an erect phallus, the goat-headed and horned Devil of nightmares. Yet, he is Pan, god of magick and initiation, concealing a smile within the horror. The arms pointing up and down signify "as above so below," *solve et coagula* (dissolve and coagulate), analysis and synthesis, the path of all knowledge. The wings symbolize the flight of the liberated soul. The flaming torch, between the horns of virility, is the awakened *Sahasrara* (or "Crown") chakra, the magical light of universal equilibrium. Baphomet is the Light Bearer, clothed in the disguise of evil.

SHIVA (Stone carving, ca. 1000 C.E., India) God of Destruction, change, transformation, annihilation, reproduction, Shiva is the third member of the *Trimurti,* the three rulers composed also of Brahma the Creator and Vishnu the Preserver. Shiva is also the patron of Yoga, specifically of Kundalini and Tantra, in which the individual ego is overwhelmed and thereby identified with universal concerns.

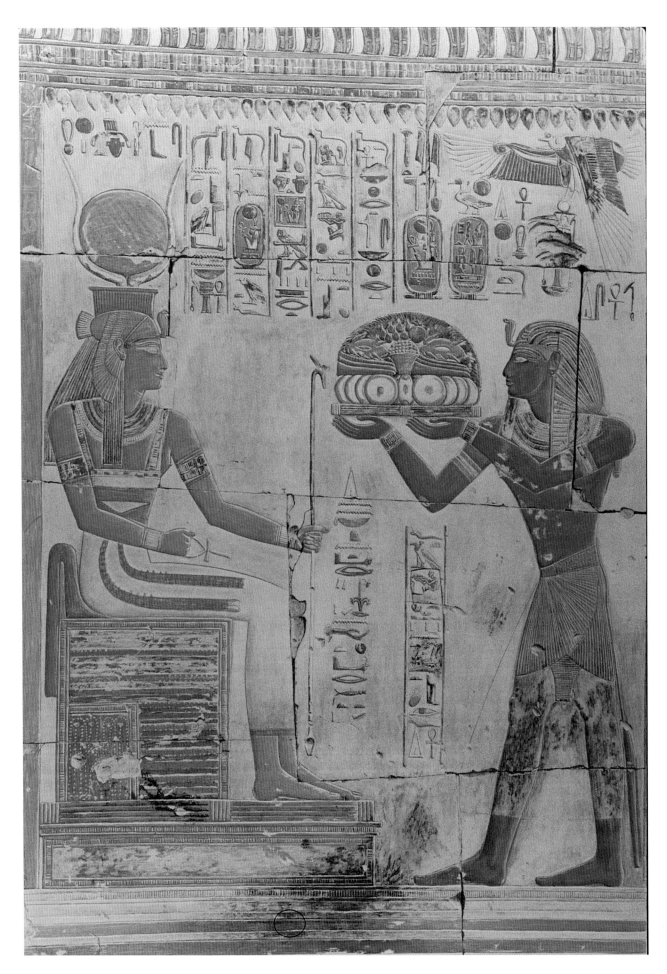

BABALON (The Thoth Tarot, painted by Frieda Harris from the design of Aleister Crowley, 1944) The Lust Card summons the image of the magically empowered female Adept in ecstatic union with her mate. It contrasts vividly in moral tone with its antecedent from St. John's Revelation, in which the goddess is described as, "the great whore . . . with whom the kings of the earth have committed fornication . . . sit[ting] upon a scarlet covered beast, full of names of blasphemy . . . having a golden cup in her hand full of abominations . . . drunken with the blood of the saints." The earlier pagan cults alluded to in this diatribe are here resuscitated. This card portrays a creative energy independent of reason and a physical-magical formula for the accomplishment of the Great Work.

OPPOSITE: ISIS (Illustration of relief from Temple of Seti I at Abydos, *Temple of Seti I at Abydos*, v. III, 1937) Isis is the greatest goddess of Egypt. She is the wife of Osiris and mother of Horus. She is particularly identified as an enchantress, whose magick was allied to the wisdom of Thoth. She is venerated as the Great Mother whose love pervaded all creation, and as the highest ideal of a loving and faithful wife and mother.

APOLLONIUS OF TYANA (Illustration, *De Divinatione et magicis praestigiis* by Jean Jacques Boissard, ca. 1615) This historical 1st century Magus has been so thoroughly identified with the magical and theurgic teachings that he has nearly attained the status of myth. A Pythagorean initiate, he traveled to India and was regarded as a wise man, healer, and wonder-worker.

OPPOSITE: THE DEATH POSTURE (Illustration by Austin Osman Spare, *The Book of Pleasure* by Austin Osman Spare, 1913) "What is there to believe, but in Self? And Self is the negation of completeness as reality. No man has seen self at any time. We are what we believe." Spare (1886–1956) was a modern Western shaman whose art and writing are filled with unconscious, atavistic complexes and stresses, evident in the tension of this self-portrait of the *Death Posture*. Yet there is a sublime meditative calm in the artist's powerful concentration.

NOSTRADAMUS (Colored drawing, 18th century, Paris) Michel de Nostra-Dame, 1503–1566, was an adviser to Catherine de Medici. A physician of Jewish descent, he was gifted with healing skills, prophetic powers, and astrological knowledge. His visionary prophesies, published in 1555 in the book entitled *Centuries*, partake of an uncanny accuracy that has baffled readers for more than 400 years. He also wrote on cosmetics, perfumes, food, and herbal recipes. He accurately foretold the circumstances of his own death.

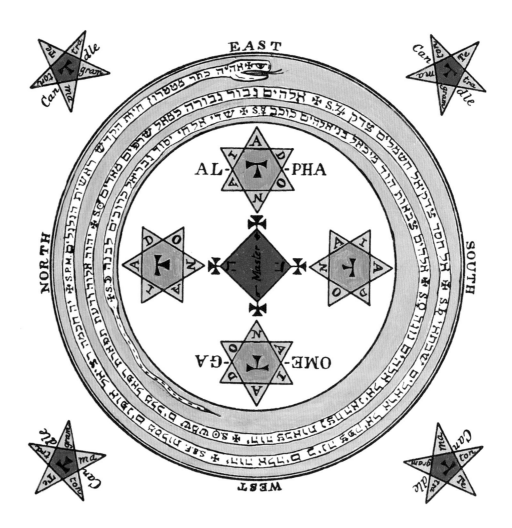

THE MAGICAL CIRCLE OF SOLOMON (Illustration, *The Book of the Goetia*, edited by Aleister Crowley, 1904, hand-colored by Nancy Wasserman) Written around the body of the Serpent are the God names of the Sephiroth of the Tree of Life, the Hebrew names of the Sephiroth, and the names of the Archangels, Angels, and Planets attributed thereto. The Words of Power surrounding the Triangle are designed to safely contain any spirit who is called into it by evocation.

OPPOSITE: **MAGE AND IMAGE and VAULT OF THE ADEPTS** (Paintings by Steffi Grant, *The Hidden Lore* by Steffi and Kenneth Grant, 1989) The ceremonial Magical Wands of the Neophyte and Adeptus Minor ceremonies of the Golden Dawn are shown with their kabbalistic attributions. The Wand is the symbol of the creative Will, dominion through concentration, and the occult element of Fire. Below are shown the floor and ceiling designs of the Vault of the Adepts, used in the Adeptus Minor ritual. The ceiling represents spiritual attainment; the floor, the demonic world to be overcome. The designs were derived from the tomb of Christian Rosenkreutz. See pages 80–82.

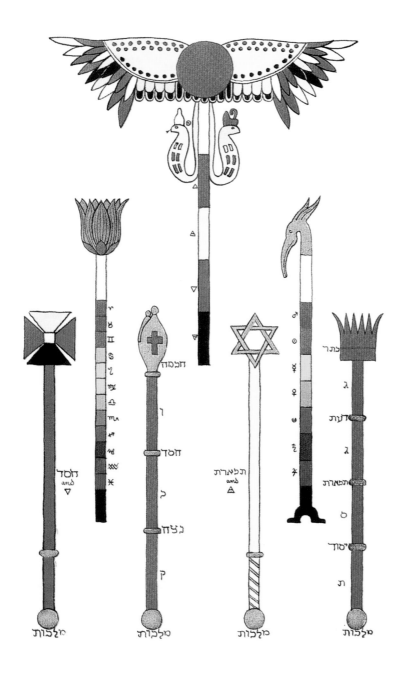

INFLUENTIAL MAGICAL TEACHERS OF THE LAST 150 YEARS

LEFT TO RIGHT: ÉLIPHAS LÉVI (1810–1875) Author of *Transcendental Magic* and *The History of Magic,* he popularized the notion that the Tarot trumps corresponded to the Hebrew letters and attempted to demonstrate the importance of the Hermetic Kabbalah.

SAMUEL LIDDELL MACGREGOR MATHERS (1854–1918) Author of *The Kabbalah Unveiled* and head of the Golden Dawn, he gave dramatic form to the Rosicrucian mythos in Western occultism. He added immeasurably to the Hermetic Kabbalah and popularized and contributed to the Enochian system of Magick.

ALEISTER CROWLEY (1875–1947) The greatest magician of the 20th century, he was a prolific writer; his literary accomplishments include *Book IV, Magick in Theory and Practice, The Book of Thoth, The Thoth Tarot,* and *The Book of the Law.* He attempted to introduce the scientific method to the techniques of mystical attainment.

HELENA PETROVNA BLAVATSKY (1831–1891) Author of *The Secret Doctrine* and *Isis Unveiled,* she was the founder of the Theosophical Society. She introduced the teachings of Indian and Buddhist philosophy to the West and popularized the concept of Hidden Masters guiding humanity.

STÉLÉ OF REVEALING (Illustration, *The Equinox*, vol. I, by Aleister Crowley, 1909–1914)
This is the funeral stélé of a 26th Dynasty priest named Ankh-f-n-khonsu (He whose life is in the Moon). He is shown addressing the throned god Ra-Hoor-Khuit. Bending over them is the Goddess of Infinite Space, Nuit. The winged solar disk is Hadit, the infinitely small point, or individuality, in relation to the all-encompassing universe. The stélé is said to be the physical link with antiquity of the revelation declared in *The Book of the Law*. Received by Aleister Crowley in 1904, the book contains moral principles applicable to the present period, popularly known as the Age of Aquarius.

SECRET SOCIETIES

Did Zanoni belong to this mystical Fraternity, who, in an earlier age, boasted of secrets of which the Philosopher's Stone was but the least; who considered themselves the heirs of all that the Chaldeans, the Magi, the Gymnosophists, and the Platonists had taught; and who differed from all the darker Sons of Magic in the virtue of their lives, the purity of their doctrines, and their insisting, as the foundation of all wisdom, on the subjugation of the senses, and the intensity of Religious Faith? —*Zanoni*, Sir Edward Bulwer Lytton[1]

The governments of the present day have to deal not merely with other governments, with emperors, kings and ministers, but also with the secret societies which have everywhere their unscrupulous agents, and can at the last moment upset all the governments' plans.

—British Prime Minister Benjamin Disraeli, 1876

TWO VERY DIFFERENT VIEWS OF SECRET SOCIETIES are revealed in the quotations above. The first describes a spiritual brotherhood pledged to Wisdom and guiding humanity toward the realm of the Infinite; the second seeks to expose the machinations of power-seekers who cloak their manipulative agendas in darkness. In addition to spiritual and political secret societies, one could add criminal secret societies such as the Mafia, or even clandestine elite military units—neither of which will be discussed here.

All secret societies share certain fundamental themes. Membership is restricted to those who have an abiding interest in the subject. Thus, a spiritual group will attract people seeking more knowledge of a particular teacher or type of practice. The student is aware of the subject matter in advance and will

THE WAR OF DREAMS (Painting by Linda Gardner, ca. 1973, colored pencils, pastel and white pencil on felt pastel paper) This exquisite painting suggests the Initiation of a Neophyte. The Invisible Masters of the Order gaze upon the scene.

approach the group for further instruction. More rarely, an individual may be "tapped" by the group because of a perceived affinity to its purpose.

In a political secret society, membership is restricted to those who share an ideological affinity with the goals the group represents. At the furthest end of the political spectrum, the mission will be revolution. Such a society will go to great lengths to defend itself. Generally there will be small semiautonomous cells working in overall concert but with cut-outs introduced at all levels to protect other members from exposure or betrayal. This type of society is represented by a contemporary group such as al-Qaeda. While Osama bin Ladin may be considered the "public face" of the organization, he is very far removed from the daily workings of its members. The infamous Weathermen of the 1960s and '70s had a similar structure. The clandestine revolutionary model was developed and perfected by Hasan-i-Sabah, leader of the Nizari Ismaili Order of Assassins between the late 11th and early 12th centuries.

On another political plane are ideological groups such as the Council on Foreign Relations, or participants in the World Economic Forum. Here we find leaders in politics, business, finance, education, and the media who may share a belief in the value of global solutions; are in high positions of authority and influence; and represent different levels of involvement with the inner circle of the group. Most members simply welcome the opportunity to associate with other well-known luminaries and are honored by being offered membership or attendence privileges. Yet, the ideology at the highest levels of such groups supports a world government—to be administered by a class of experts and planners, entrusted with running centrally organized social and political institutions. Although members may be persuaded to add their considerable voices to certain transnational political and economic policies, they may not be as supportive (or even aware) of the long-range ambitions of the inner circle. While these groups quite often hold their meetings in secret, their membership lists are a matter of public record. It is the central agenda that is disguised.

Adam Weishaupt, whose portrait opens this chapter, founded the Bavarian Illuminati in 1776. The Illuminati are perceived by many as spanning the chasm between the spiritual and the political secret society. Often credited (or blamed) for influencing the French Revolution in 1787, the Illuminati taught a doctrine of social and political liberation that hinged on the equality of man, the embrace of rationalism, and the denial of crown and church as the legitimate institutions for the regulation of social and moral values. The bitterness of

life in Europe at this time—when church and state monopolized resources and often acted in an irresponsible manner toward the citizenry—created widespread resentment among all classes. While the views of the Illuminati may sound quite advanced for the time, the European revolutions they are believed to have encouraged degenerated into brutal bloodbaths whose singular lack of moral compass was appalling.

The type of secret society we will be discussing and illustrating in these pages is the spiritual. The underlying message of spiritual secret societies is discussed in the chapter on Initiation (see pages 35–53). All spiritual secret societies subscribe to the Gnostic Mysteries; that is, they posit a Divine Wisdom that is attainable by the individual through his own efforts, perhaps aided by the guidance of more experienced brethren.

Among the most influential spiritual secret societies are the historical Knights Templar, the Freemasons, the Hermetic Order of the Golden Dawn, the Ordo Templi Orientis (O.T.O.), and A∴A∴. The Templars were founded ca. 1118 in Jerusalem during the Crusades. The Order introduced a new concept to Christianity—the union of warrior and monk. It rapidly achieved wide acceptance and acclaim. Two hundred years later, the Order was crushed amid charges of heresy, blasphemy, and treason. Freemasonry is the best known secret society. The first evidence of the initiation of a speculative Mason (one who was neither an architect nor a builder) is a diary entry by scholar and scientist Elias Ashmole in 1646. The Golden Dawn was founded in London in 1888. The Order's esoteric synthesis remains the dominant intellectual curriculum for English-speaking students of the Mystery Traditions. Ordo Templi Orientis and A∴A∴ are two modern magical Orders working in harmony with the New Aeon revelations of *The Book of the Law*, given through Aleister Crowley in 1904. The Golden Dawn and O.T.O. are further discussed in the chapters on Initiation and Magick.

In the Preliminary Lection of *Liber LXI vel Causae*, Aleister Crowley, later the Praemonstrator of A∴A∴ and Outer Head of O.T.O., stated the following regarding a true magical order.

2. In all systems of religion is to be found a system of Initiation, which may be defined as the process by which a man comes to learn that unknown Crown.

3. Though none can communicate either the knowledge or the power to achieve this, which we may call the Great Work, it is yet possible for initiates to guide others.

4. Every man must overcome his own obstacles, expose his own illusions. Yet others may assist him to do both,

and they may enable him altogether to avoid many of the false paths, leading no whither, which tempt the weary feet of the uninitiated pilgrim. They can further insure that he is duly tried and tested, for there are many who think themselves to be Masters who have not even begun to tread the Way of Service that leads thereto.[2]

Dion Fortune, a member of the Stella Matutina, supports Crowley's statement that the real work takes place within the individual.

It is up this ladder that the aspirant climbs toward the light, and his progress depends on none but himself, for even the Order upon this earth is but the gateway that leads into the Unseen: it is from the Great Initiator alone that he can take his initiation, and that initiation is not given in the flesh or by the flesh.[3]

In a spiritual secret society, the primary relationship one is forming is with one's own Higher Self. The goal is the elevation of individual consciousness. So if the work is individual, and if it is accomplished in private, what is the purpose of membership in a secret society?

There are several different advantages to be gained from such membership. The most obvious is the opportunity to associate with more advanced practitioners in one's chosen field of study. One is very likely to meet such a person or people because of the social setting one has chosen.

Second, a true secret society is founded by an Adept who is advancing a specific teaching. As discussed in the Initiation chapter, these Adepts are conceived as working in conjunction with Intelligences at a higher level of consciousness. The joining and swearing of Oaths to such an Order completes a type of spiritual circuitry between the aspirant and the inner source of the teaching to which he or she aspires.

Furthermore, although all practice is individual, the nature of life is such that the sum is often greater than its parts. Thus, in a group of individuals—each of whom brings the strength of his or her own inner work to a common purpose—the results can be more dramatic than for a lone operator. There is more psychic energy available to all if each member is spiritually fit and capable of contributing to the whole.

Membership in a secret society allows one to be immersed in an environment in which others of a similar mind are working to improve themselves. Therefore social contact generally remains focused on the mutual interests that brought everyone together in the first place. This tends to encourage greater familiarity with the chosen subject matter and can be an incentive to greater individual work.

Likewise, the association with others at various levels of spiritual development creates a pressure cooker atmosphere that can challenge the ego in profoundly meaningful ways. One's assets may be applauded by one's associates; one's failings will certainly be criticized. Most important, the often-erroneous thinking that is a common problem for those on the spiritual path will be questioned. When an initiate shares his revelations with other members of the group, he or she shouldn't be too surprised to meet skeptical eyes. People who are psychologically strong enough to expose themselves to this type of scrutiny tend to become even stronger and more well-balanced.

Finally, the simple realities involved in helping to maintain the society tend to keep one grounded. (It is much harder to imagine oneself the chosen savior of humanity when it's your turn to mop the Temple floor.)

There are also pitfalls to belonging to such a society. There is often a group ego in which a certain snobbery takes hold because one is a "member." This is common enough among groups as mundane as baseball teams or college fraternities. In the case of a spiritual secret society, the arrogance can assume an even more self-righteous cast. After all, those within the sacred fold stand upon the threshold of great revelation, while the common rabble have not even awakened to the question. "As the civilized man is to the savage, so is the Adept to the average man."[4]

Members may also mistake intense socializing for spiritual work. For example, after group rituals, especially those performed on a regular basis, a sense of familiarity and repetition can mislead a person into thinking he is accomplishing something by discussing ideas or sharing fellowship with other members. However, instead of going out after a ritual to express one's thoughts over dinner or drinks, a period of private meditation or individual study might be of far greater value.

A third drawback to secret societies is that some people can more easily manipulate others because of the sense of trust and aspiration a younger member brings to the process. Predators may flourish in such environments unless they are carefully and consistently weeded out by higher authority. This is an especially disturbing and dangerous issue because it is often necessary to submit to discipline and guidance to reach the next level of one's spiritual pursuit. In theory, fellow members should be allies in one's spiritual growth. A member naturally tends to "look up" to those with more experience, more status in the group, people in positions of leadership. But it is important to remember that even the more advanced member has an ego and is pursuing his or her individual progress on the Path—which involves making mistakes. A person in leadership can—by exercising insufficient introspection—injure another because that leader is not willing to fearlessly plumb the true depths of his own motivation.

To avoid some of the dangers inherent in secret societies, the most important thing the seeker can bring to the experience is confidence in his or her own judgment and intuition. If something seems wrong, get out. Remember, that something actually *might be* wrong, and your decision at this early stage could save much grief. There will be an internal conflict because you will have a set of aspirations based on your understanding of the Work, and you will feel the group *should be* right for you. However, there is a converse to the old truism, "When the student is ready the teacher appears." It is this, "When the student is not ready, false teachers may attempt to impersonate real teachers."

If any attempt is made to elicit or promote sexual contact in order to help one "advance upon the Path"— and there is no mutual attraction involved—you should immediately take your leave. This is one of the oldest tricks in the book and is a despicable profanation of a Holy force. Similarly, if money is requested to "advance the Work," one might be better advancing to the exit. Now obviously practicality is involved here. All groups have expenses. Yet, no one is entitled to the fruit of another's labor not freely offered.

The main question that is always raised about secret societies concerns secrecy itself. If there is nothing to hide, why should people cloak their behavior in darkness? One needs to look at this from the point of view of practicality. How can serious people make progress in their chosen field of study if their efforts are continually dissipated by casual onlookers, the merely curious, the temperamentally unfit, and the dilettante? Think of special interest groups of any kind. What binds the members together is common purpose and a common focus.

Now add the elements of spiritual and occult power. If one doesn't believe there is power in magical practices, it is better to avoid joining groups whose purpose is to cultivate that power. Otherwise, one should respect and appreciate the efforts of those who seek to guard and protect spiritual power from the unworthy or morally corrupt. In the novel *Zanoni*, quoted at the chapter opening, Bulwer Lytton explains that secret societies hold their teachings close to protect the larger community from the misuse of psychic power. Zanoni's fellow Adept admonishes the aspirant (later found unworthy) in the following words:

> "Dost thou think," said Mejnour, "that I would give to the mere pupil, whose qualities are not yet tried, powers that might change the face of the social world? The last secrets are entrusted only to him of whose virtue the Master is convinced."[5]

Another reason for secrecy is the nature of the states of mind that are attained in group ritual. Magick is a dangerous pursuit. Its history is littered with catastrophic consequences and failures due to the peculiar character of psychic energy. Those who seek to enter the sacred space "between the worlds" through a successful ritual do so at their own risk. The largely uncharted regions of the universe of the mind—in which Truth resides, guarded by Fierce Protectors—leave the Adept vulnerable in direct proportion to the power invoked. An untrained or undisciplined breach of the Circle could be fatal. These are strong words that may sound melodramatic: but they are true. To help guard against such danger, the company of a sworn body of tested allies is the best protection. The magical Circle is drawn to define a controlled environment.

A final thought. I have spent my adult life within the milieu of spiritual secret societies. (These days they're listed on the Internet.) In preparing the photo essay that follows, I was humbled once again by the warmth and cooperation shown by many friends, associates, and total strangers of my own and other organizations. Nearly all of the people with whom I communicated were generous of their time, helpful beyond measure, kind in their persons, and individually committed to the Great Work. At the end of the day, that may be the most important statement that can be made about the true value of spiritual secret societies.

OPPOSITE: SHAMAN BAYIR RINCHINOV (Photo by Alexander Khantaev, 2000, Siberia) This Buryat Adept is pictured at the climax of an invocation of an *Ongon*, or ancestral spirit. The photo conveys, better than do words, the power and otherwordliness of a real magical ceremony. A controlled environment is critical for the psychic safety of the operator, who will be sure to exclude those who are not carefully vetted. The need for secret societies in the pursuit of esoteric disciplines is a practical concern. Tried and tested allies, sworn by Oath to the work of the group, can, in theory, be regarded as trustworthy.

THE FALL OF ACRE (Painting by Papety, Dominique, ca. 1845) One of the final battles of the Knights Templar during the Crusades. When Acre fell, on May 28, 1291, the Christian presence in the Holy Land was ended. The Templars fled to Cyprus.

OPPOSITE ABOVE: KNEELING CRUSADER (Latin psalter, ca. 1175–ca. 1200) The intense piety of the Holy Warrior is illustrated as the armed and armored knight prays before a battle.

OPPOSITE BELOW: TEMPLAR SEAL (34 mm, private collection) The two knights riding on one horse (obverse) symbolized the Order's embrace of poverty. The al-Aqsa mosque (reverse) was the original home of the Order awarded to them by King Baldwin II of Jerusalem.

GEORGE WASHINGTON AS MASTER OF HIS FREEMASONIC LODGE (Painting by Hattie Burdette, 1932) Washington was Charter Master of Lodge No. 22 while he served as President. Benjamin Franklin, Alexander Hamilton, Paul Revere, John Paul Jones, and the Marquis de Lafayette were all Masons, as were 13 other presidents including both Roosevelts. Masonic values include freedom of thought and worship, universal tolerance, freedom of association, the spirit of open inquiry, brotherhood, equality before God and the law, individual rights, and the consent of the governed.

THE GREAT SEAL OF THE UNITED STATES was designed by a committee composed of Thomas Jefferson, Benjamin Franklin, John Adams, and antiquarian Eugene Simitieré, chosen at the signing of the Declaration of Independence. They proposed the motto *E Pluribus Unum* (From the Many One) and the All Seeing Eye design. The phrases *Novus Ordo Seculorum* (New Order of the Ages) and *Annuit Coeptis* (He Favors Our Undertaking) were added in 1782. The Eye in the Triangle was considered such an overtly Masonic symbol that a die was not struck until 1935, when Freemason Henry Wallace suggested to Freemason Franklin Roosevelt that both sides of the Seal appear, for the first time, on the dollar bill.

OPPOSITE: TRACING BOARD OF THE FIRST DEGREE (Hand-painted on wood by J. Bowring, 1819) The Mason undertakes the ascent of Jacob's Ladder in his journey to the Truth. The tracing board design is a symbolic visual representation of the knowledge conveyed in the degree.

THE VAULT OF THE ADEPTS OF THE HEREMETIC ORDER OF THE GOLDEN DAWN (Photo by Chic Cicero)

This is the primary Temple and Initiation Chamber of the Second Order of the Golden Dawn, the *R.R. et A.C.* or *Rosae Rubae et Aurae Crucis* (Red Rose and Golden Cross). Its design is based on a description of the Tomb of Christian Rosenkreutz, founder of the Rosicrucian Order, contained within the mysterious pamphlet, *Fama Fraternitatis* published in 1614. The *Fama* announced the discovery of the Tomb, proclaimed the existence of the Rosicrucian Brotherhood, and created a European-wide fascination with the ideal of a society of enlightened Adepts guiding humanity.

S. L. MacGregor Mathers, a founder and later head of the Golden Dawn, is credited as the genius behind the adaptation of that legend to this extraordinary kabbalistic design. The Temple pictured here was constructed by Chic Cicero and consecrated by Israel Regardie in Columbus, Georgia in 1982.

The Vault of the Adepts symbolizes the sacred Mountain of Initiation or Abiegnus, also pictured in the Rosicrucian diagram reproduced on page 50. The floor and ceiling designs of the Vault are shown in more detail on page 67. The complete symbol of the Rose Cross, worn over the heart of the Chief Adept during the Adeptus Minor initiation ritual, may be found on page 53. The ritual itself celebrates the Mystery of the Crucifixion and the story of the Rosicrucian Brotherhood.

The Vault is a seven-sided room, each side being under the dominion of one of the seven ancient planets shown on the ceiling design on page 67. Each wall measures five feet wide by eight feet high and contains forty squares painted in a series of revolving elemental colors. Each square displays either planetary, zodiacal, alchemical, elemental, or cherubic iconography. Properly painted, the complementary colors of each of these 280 squares vibrate and "flash" with an intensity that serves to accentuate the stored energy of the Temple. One might describe it metaphorically as a spiritual cyclotron, in which psychic energy is both stimulated and intensified.

See the following photo spread for a detail of the Altar and Pastos with further description.

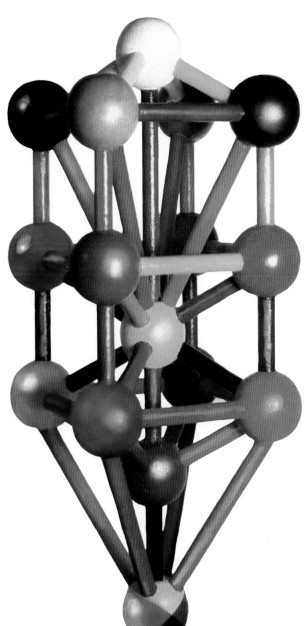

OPPOSITE ABOVE: **Detail of the ALTAR AND PASTOS WITHIN THE VAULT OF THE ADEPTS** (Photo by Chic Cicero) The figure painted on the lid of the Pastos stands in the *Tiphareth* position of the Tree of Life. He is identified as Christian Rosenkreutz, founder of the Order and the "Occult Christ." The Chief Adept takes the god form of Rosencreutz during Second Order initiation ceremonies. The head of the Pastos faces East, the direction of the dawning of the light. It occupies the center of the Vault, the point of balanced Force. Above it is the Circular Altar. The Hebrew letter *Shin,* symbol of Spirit, is placed in the midst of the Four Elements (represented by the four discs with their Cherubic icons). The *Shin* symbol is placed directly under the Rose in the center of the ceiling design. On the Altar stands a carved Rose Cross, the Chain of Discipline, the Dagger of Analysis, the Cup of Intuition, and the Crook and Flail of Sacred Kingship. The circumference of the Altar is inscribed with a proclamation of devotion to the Inner Christ and quotations from the *Fama.*

LEFT: **THE THREE-DIMENSIONAL TREE OF LIFE** (Built by Dr. Robert Wang) This magnificent model follows the design by Mathers as described in his Golden Dawn paper, "The Tree of Life Projected in a Solid Sphere."

BELOW: **THE GREEK CROSS OF THE GOLDEN DAWN** (Painting by Nancy Wasserman) This equal armed cross is composed of 13 squares—the Sun in the center of the 12 astrological signs. Each arm displays the triplicities discussed in the Astrology chapter: namely Water signs on top, Fire signs on the right, Air signs on the left, and Earth signs on the bottom. It represents Spirit (the Sun) in the midst of the Four Elements acting as a redemptive and informative force.

OPPOSITE BELOW: Two original designs based on the traditional symbolism of the Tree of Life.

FAR LEFT: **THE UNICURSAL HEXAGRAM** (computer art by James Wasserman) The colors of the *Sephiroth* at the center of the Tree of Life, including *Daath,* are blended along the Paths with the Sun of *Tiphareth* in the center. See page 28.

NEAR LEFT: **THE LIVING TREE** (designed by Frater Achad and painted by Will Ransom) In 1923, Charles Stansfeld Jones, Frater Achad, had a vision of the Tree of Life with its roots in the Infinitely Small, and its branches extending toward the Infinitely Great. He also became aware of the centrality of the Vesica shape in these Mysteries.

THE PORTAL OF THE SECOND ORDER (Painting by Major General J. F. C. Fuller, 1909) This powerful image includes the cherubic angels of the four elements, the Ouroboros serpent, the elevenfold Crown, and the Holy Names of the Divine. In addition to his esoteric work, Fuller is recognized as one of the most important military theoreticians of the twentieth century.

OPPOSITE ABOVE: GNOSTIC MASS ALTAR (Photo by Illia Tulloch) Crowley described the Gnostic Mass as the central ritual, public and private of the O.T.O. It is celebrated on a regular basis worldwide by members of the Order. This one was built by Swirling Star Oasis.

OPPOSITE LOWER LEFT: O.T.O. LAMEN (Hand painted by Aleister Crowley) The Lamen of the Order is enclosed within the Vesica Piscis, wherein radiates the Eye in the Triangle, which sends forth the Dove to drop the substance of the Holy Spirit into the Cup of the Holy Grail.

OPPOSITE LOWER RIGHT: THE ADEPT IN THE MYSTIC PORTAL making the Sign of Silence. He stands between the two pillars of Osiris, and beneath the Winged Solar Disk of the Mysteries.

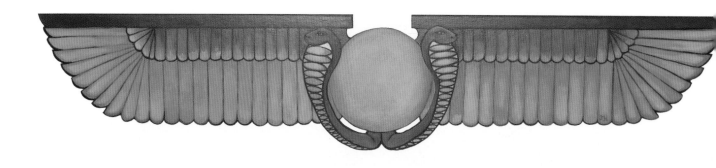

TOP OF PAGE: **WINGED SOLAR DISK** (John and Merrie Hodges, 1970, restored and completed by Linda Gardner, ca. 1993) May this powerful symbol of the soul, free to soar through the Empyrean realm, serve as a prayer for the well-being of departed friends.

ABOVE: **CALIPH HYMENAEUS ALPHA, O.T.O.** (Photo by Herman Slater, ca. 1980) Grady Louis McMurtry (1918–1985) joined the Ordo Templi Orientis in Los Angeles in 1941. As a young American soldier during WWII, he became a personal student and friend of Aleister Crowley in London. Crowley authorized him to take over the entire work of the Order in the event of an emergency, which McMurtry determined faced the Order in 1969. Under his leadership, the O.T.O. was reborn and grew into a worldwide organization active in over 50 countries.

SOME ADEPTS OF THE TWENTIETH CENTURY

LEFT TO RIGHT: **HARRY SMITH** (1923–1991) Filmmaker, ethnomusicologist, anthropologist, painter, teacher, and occultist, Harry won a Lifetime Grammy award for his contribution to American Folk Music. He was an enormous influence in the lives of the many people he touched.

DR. ISRAEL REGARDIE (1907–1985) The primary preserver and transmitter of the Magical teachings of both the Golden Dawn and Aleister Crowley. His courage and dedication in the face of ridicule, criticism, and enforced obscurity places every modern practitioner of Western Esotericism in his debt.

FRIEDA LADY HARRIS (née Bloxham, 1877–1962) Wife of Sir Percy Harris M.P., Lady Harris was a visionary artist who painted the Thoth Tarot under the direction of Aleister Crowley. Their work on the project extended for five years. See Tarot chapter to view the Major Arcana of this seminal deck.

JOHN WHITESIDE PARSONS (1914–1952) Chemical engineer and explosives expert, Jack Parsons helped found the Jet Propulsion Laboratory in Pasadena, California. A crater on the Moon is named after him in honor of his work on the solid fuel rocket that propelled mankind into space. He joined O.T.O. in 1941 and briefly served as Master of Agapé Lodge.

SEXUALITY

Let him kiss me with the kisses of his mouth. . . . My beloved is white and ruddy, the chiefest among ten thousand. His head is as the most fine gold . . . his belly is as bright ivory overlaid with sapphires. His legs are as pillars of marble, set upon sockets of fine gold . . . yea, he is altogether lovely."

How beautiful are thy feet . . . the joints of thy thighs are like jewels . . . Thy navel is like a round goblet which wanteth not liquor: thy belly is like an heap of wheat set about with lilies. Thy two breasts are like two young roes that are twins. . . . How fair and how pleasant art thou, O love, for delights!

Set me as a seal upon thine heart, as a seal upon thine arm: for love is strong as death. Many waters cannot quench love, neither can floods drown it.

—*The Song of Solomon*[1]

SEX IS THE MIRROR OF DIVINE UNITY manifested as polarity—duality seeking its counterpart on earth, "divided for love's sake, for the chance of union."[2] Lust is the key to the universe. In terms of the theory of correspondence, the longing of Yin for Yang is the desire of the electron for the proton. This is the force that sustains the atom and thereby creation.

The world is a composite of positive and negative, light and dark, male and female, birth and death. The Sun is the Lord of Day and Heaven; the Moon is the Lady of Night and subconsciousness. United in the Mystical Marriage, they form the Child, the human race, the inheritor of both qualities. The union of Mars and Venus, War and Love, produces Harmony. Beauty cannot exist without contraries. Opposites produce concord.

The Female is the Lover, the Friend and Sister, the Virgin Mother, the Holy Whore, the Fierce Protectoress and Destructive Demoness, ever dancing upon

LEDA & THE SWAN (Painting, School of Leonardo da Vinci, 1510–1515, Italy)

the bodies of Her devotees. She is all things to all men, and yet ever concealed within herself. The Male is Pan (root of the word "panic"), the frenzied, lust-filled Madman, the Lover, Father, Brother, Friend, the Killer and Protector, the Provider. The union of the two in the act of love, the Mystical Marriage, is the apotheosis of the race. For herein we become as God, sharing in the divine power of creation through our bodies. And like God, we can populate the universe in our own image. The sexual act is always regarded as either sacred or profane because of its intrinsic power. Sexuality is included within the moral canon of every culture because it is the most basic, life-giving, race-sustaining act on earth.

Sex is the one subject in this book of which every reader has knowledge, the one subject of our inquiry that has universal relevance. For sex is the great equalizer. Everything that lives partakes of a sexual nature, whether plants, animals, or human beings. We began through the sexual union of our parents and have all dealt with the sexual issue in our lives. There are no exceptions and there is no escape.

Does the occultist's view of sex differ? Why should sex be included in a book of esoteric symbols? The answer is that sex is the basis of the Mystery Traditions as well as of life on earth; sex is the ultimate symbolic unifying agent of all the disciplines discussed here.

The occultist perceives the basic life force as a bio-electric energy known the world over as *kundalini*. Kundalini is sexual energy. The management of this energy is the root of Yoga and meditation; the raising and directing of this energy is the purpose of Magick; its purification, the goal of Alchemy; its symbolic descriptions are contained in the concepts of Astrology and Kabbalah; the unification of all aspects of theory and practice is Initiation. The conscious sexual act is the simplest and most pure symbol of the love of the divine for its creation.

Therefore, the right use of sexual energy is a primary concern of the practicing occultist. The esoteric teachings regarding sexuality that have been developed over the millennia and in many different civilizations may be called "tantric." The best known traditions are probably the Hindu and Buddhist. Both have a rich iconography, expressed in ornate temples and other artwork of exquisite and openly sensual beauty. Chinese Taoist alchemical practices are centuries old, with elaborate procedures in the use and development of sexual energies for increased physical health and occult power.

Early Egyptian use of esoteric sexuality is clearly demonstrated by its iconography and myths. The sexual activity of the gods results in both procreation and the altering of the world. There is a Jewish tradition of assisting God in his nuptials with the *Shekinah* (the bride of the patriarchal Judaic God). On the Sabbath, a couple's ritualized lovemaking helps God and the Shekinah sustain the manifestation of the world. Ecstatic religious worship is integral to Hasidism, and the sexual nature of the universe is clearly acknowledged in the Jewish Kabbalah. Islamic culture has a highly developed tantric practice within the mystical Sufi tradition. Likewise, there has always been a healthy sensual aspect to Islam, fundamentalism notwithstanding.

Gnostics in the early centuries of the common era taught a great many shades of sexual behavior, ranging from ascetic to sensual, depending on the specific group. Christianity has maintained a rigidly antisexual stance (thanks in no small degree to St. Paul), despite whatever hints or suggestions of a sexual teaching might be offered by the unique relationship between Jesus and Mary Magdalene. If there is a positive mainstream Christian attitude toward sexuality, it is demonstrated by the recognition of marriage as a sacrament. Any other sexual religious experimentation within the Christian tradition must be found among its heresies—tainted by blasphemy, the bastard child of repression and guilt. In some instances, deeply religious Christians have experienced mystical transformation through sexual union and have elevated sex to a divine status in the worship of their Christ. Often as not, these periodic outcroppings of Christian tantra were literally crushed. One most brutal example is the Albigensian Crusades of the 13th century. The Albigensians or Cathars lived in the French and Spanish Pyrenees, where they practiced a heretical form of worship that may have included sexual doctrines along with their antipapist sentiments. On the Pope's orders, thousands were killed. "Kill them all, God will know His own" is said to have been uttered by the papal legate in charge of the campaign.

The most powerful repositories of the sexual religious tradition in the West are pre-Christian Paganism, and later Witchcraft, Magick, and Alchemy. Here all symbols point to the use of sex for the accomplishment of mystical goals. The hidden nature of the Occult allowed for the survival of an Esoteric Tradition in the West, despite ages of repressive political power wielded by the Church.

The repression of the sexual nature, which may well be the predominant cultural theme of Judeo-Christian society, has led to a disturbing and debased modern morass. The hysteria of Western sexual attitudes might be comical if it were not so deeply rooted in, and productive of, human agony. The mass media overflows with a leering sexual obsession that consumes both editors and readers. Scandals, innuendoes, lascivious and raging fantasies, sexual crimes, child molestation, pornography, censorship, jealousy, exploitation—these symptomatic pathologies scream from every newsstand and television screen. Meanwhile a depersonalized, mechanistic, self-indulgent model of soulless sexuality is endlessly paraded before a hopelessly consumerized populace: Sexual liberation indeed! This is an abnormal situation—sadly characteristic of Eros distorted.

An alternative viewpoint is expressed by the immortal William Blake in his *Marriage of Heaven and Hell:* "the whole creation will . . . appear infinite and holy, whereas it now appears finite & corrupt. *This will come to pass by an improvement of sensual enjoyment.* But first the notion that man has a body distinct from his soul is to be expunged . . . If the doors of perception were cleansed every thing would appear to man as it is, Infinite."[3] [Italics added.]

Humanity needs to respect this precious, natural drive and to heal the sexual self. Marselio Ficino, the Renaissance Hermeticist mentioned in the chapter on Magick, saw pleasure itself as a worthwhile philosophical end. He wrote that the joys of the senses foreshadow heavenly delights. Ecstasy is beyond Image. Only within Being may one seek it.

The ecstasy implicit in the sexual-religious experience is conveyed in a passage attributed to the archetypal Goddess of Infinite Space in *The Book of the Law,* a modern tantric text by Aleister Crowley. The Goddess proclaims, "But to love me is better than all things: if under the night-stars in the desert thou presently burnest mine incense before me, invoking me with a pure heart, and the Serpent flame therein, thou shalt come a little to lie in my bosom. For one kiss wilt thou then be willing to give all; but whoso gives one particle of dust shall lose all in that hour."[4]

The joy central to the experience of Union with God has been passionately expressed in the world's mystical poetry and myth. The most clear reflection of the state of Divine Union available to our race as a whole is contained in the personal sexual experience. For sex offers the opportunity for a temporary obscuration of our normal limited ego-consciousness and the possibility of union with our partner, and thence to the sensual reality of the God and Goddess. Edgar Wind in *Pagan Mysteries in the Renaissance* states that being possessed in love by a god is the highest form of death.[5] The annihilation of the personal egoic envelope, and union with a deeper reality, is the key to the tantric sexual experience. The Sufi master Sheikh Abdullah Ansari has written:

> O Lord, intoxicate me with the wine
>   Of Thy love.
> Place the chains of Thy slavery on
>   My feet;
> Make me empty of all but Thy love,
> And in it destroy me and bring me
>   Back to life.
> The hunger Thou has awakened, culminates
>   In fulfillment.[6]

A Brief Word on Practice

Several practical comments are in order for a better understanding of sexual yoga as a means of attainment. The first is that sexual yoga is a cooperative discipline, right attitude being necessary for the attainment of the heights of sexual ecstasy. One learns to perceive one's partner as a channel for, and vehicle of, the divine, and to worship that manifestation in its fullest sense—passionately: "Enflame thyself in prayer."[7] The act of love should induce the greatest heightening of all elements of the self and the senses. Then all is abandoned in a climax of ecstatic union with the Divine. Experience and practice are the key.

In the larger view of tantra, all consensual acts between adults are perfectly appropriate to induce religious sexual ecstasy. "There is no act or passion that shall not be a hymn in mine honour."[8] Individual variations in the sexual theme are most important; all aspects of our sexual lives will ultimately weave themselves into the beautiful tapestry of the world sexual pattern.

We have sought to join images here to show the multiplicity of the sexual experience—concentration and frenzy, monogamy and promiscuity, romantic love and physical passion, simplistic joy and occult technique. "Come forth, o children, under the stars, & take your fill of love!"[9]

VENUS OF WILLENDORF (Limestone statue, ca. 25,000 B.C.E., Europe) This Upper Paleolithic female figure represents woman in her role as life-giver, sustainer, and nourisher. The lack of features of individuality in the face conveys an archetypal sense of the Female beyond the veil of her ego.

TLAZOLTEOTL GIVING BIRTH (Ceremonial statue, aplite speckled with garnets, 15th century, Mexico) She is the image of woman reclaiming her power through the act of consciously giving birth. The Aztecs accorded special respect to a woman who died in child-birth and honored her as a warrior. Some of the most demanding Native American and Samoan rituals are said to inspire men to the courage of a birthing woman. One who knows the cost, as well as the miracle, of creation places a greater value on life.

THE MADONNA OF THE SACRED COAT
(Painting by C. B. Chambers, ca. 1890, New York) A gift to the author, this lovely image of the Virgin suggests the Mary Magdalene archetype, as well as Mary the Mother, capturing the multifaceted nature of the Goddess in an intriguing manner.

LILITH (Sumerian terra-cotta plaque, ca. 2300 B.C.E.)

Wild cats will meet hyenas there,
The satyrs will call to each other,
There Lilith shall repose
And find her a place of rest. (Isaiah 34:14)

Raphael Patai in *The Hebrew Goddess* writes, "No she-demon has ever achieved as fantastic a career as Lilith who started out from the lowliest origins, was a failure as Adam's intended wife, became the paramour of lascivious spirits, rose to be the bride of Samael the demon King, ruled as the Queen of Zemargad and Sheba, and finally ended up as the consort of God himself."

THE BIRTH OF VENUS (Painting by Sandro Botticelli, ca. 1485) The sensual essence of Venus rules erotic and romantic love. She was born from the foam of the sea near the island of Cythera. The foam arose from the genitals of Uranus, which Cronus flung into the sea after castrating him. Venus's Greek name, Aphrodite, means "foam born." She was carried to land on a scallop shell, guided by the gentle southern winds. The Goddess of Spring rushed to clothe her as she stepped ashore, whereupon flowers fell from heaven.

OPPOSITE: SEKHMET (Temple relief, Egypt) The lion-headed Sekhmet is the Goddess of Vengeance and Battle and punisher of the damned—those who have revolted against moral law—in the Underworld. Sekhmet is also the goddess of female sexual heat, an aspect of Hathor, the Egyptian Venus. Devouring, fierce, and protective of her offspring, she is a member of the Great Triad of Memphis, the wife of Ptah (discoverer of fire) and the mother of Nefetum (the Greek Prometheus).

Bonfils
10

212 - Reine Isis - Egypte

OFFERING TO MIN (Drawing of Temple wall, Denderah, by artists of the Napoleonic expedition, ca. 1799) The pharaoh is making an offering of lettuce to Min, god of fertility and virility. This plant was believed to be an aphrodisiac. The ceremony of climbing the pole for Min is taking place between the deity and the worshiper. Min was identified by the Greeks with Pan.

FANCIFUL SYMBOL OF PHALLIC WORSHIP (Roman bas-relief, ca. 2nd century, reproduced in *The Worship of the Generative Powers* by Thomas Wright, 1866) This relief was once located atop a pilaster in the amphitheater of the city of Nîmes in southern France.

SHIVA LINGAM (Stone statue, India) The sacred image of the phallus of Shiva, conjoined with the vagina or *yoni* of his consort, is common throughout India. Their union is venerated as the source of birth, fertility, and reproduction on all planes.

ITHYPHALLIC SHIVA (Statue, Katmandu, Nepal, ca. 17th century)

SATYR (Sculpture by Andrea Briosco Riccio, early 16th century) A companion of Pan, god of the flock and of nature. This boisterous, life-affirming spirit of unabashed and joyful sexuality is an archetypal force that, sadly, has been weakened in modern Western civilization.

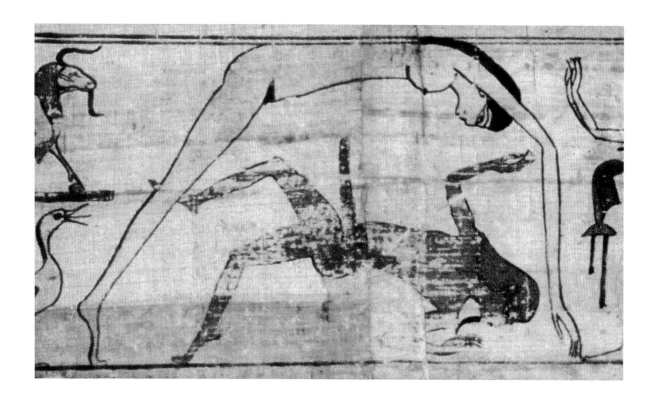

SHIVA AND SHAKTI (Khajuraho Temple complex, ca. 1000 C.E., India) This North Indian temple is replete with sculptures representing the mythical love-making of the Hindu gods, the creative powers of the universe depicted in highly meditative and erotic images of sexual union.

OPPOSITE ABOVE: NUT AND GEB (*Papyrus of Tamenill*, ca. 1000 B.C.E., Egypt) The Sky Goddess and Her Earth God brother were originally locked in an embrace, until separated by the Air God Shu.

OPPOSITE BELOW: JUPITER SEDUCING OLYMPIA (Painting by Guilio Romano, ca. 1520) This tantalizing mythological erotic scene of the Roman gods at their love-play leaves little need for comment.

A BACCHANAL (Painting by Nicholas Poussin, 1630) This painting portrays the ecstatic revels of the God of the Vine. Bacchus, the Greek Dionysus, connotes the wild frenzy of alcoholic intoxication and the sensual, sexual nature. Equally, he represents the spiritual intoxication of the Word. Stripped of the accretions of the ego, the soul in ultimate abandon to the embraces of its Lord is enthralled in the passionate rapture of union.

OPPOSITE: VENUS AND MARS UNITED BY LOVE (Painting by Paolo Veronese, 1576) Mars is the warlike, aggressive archetype of male sexuality; Venus, the beautiful, sensual archetype of female sexuality. They are shown here united by the playful Cupid, the personification of Love, who is tying their legs together. The union of opposites produces Harmony.

SUN AND MOON BATTLE (Manuscript illumination, *Aurora consurgens,* late 14th century) In this alchemical manuscript, the mystical marriage is represented by the combat of Sun and Moon, male and female. Each bears a shield with the emblem of the other, indicating that each aspect contains its own opposite. Alchemically, this image represents the battle of the fixed and the volatile, the sulphur and mercury of the philosophers.

THE LOVER'S CARD (*The Thoth Tarot,* painted by Frieda Harris from the design of Aleister Crowley, 1944) The Alchemical Marriage depicted in this card shows Cupid—the libido—blind and inspired. The hooded wisdom figure, Mercury, blesses the Hermetic marriage. The black king with the golden crown weds the white queen with the silver crown. He is accompanied by the red lion; she, by the white eagle. The white child carries the queen's cup and roses, the black child holds the king's lance and club. The winged Orphic egg is the result of the Marriage, and the glyph of the offspring of all male/female coupling.

SOLAR ECLIPSE I (Painting by Thaedra MabraKhan, 1991) This painting is one of a series of five. It shows multiple symbols that include a strong influence from the mythology of the South American Mayan culture. The union of the central Sun and Moon forms the *Vesica Piscis,* the geometrical representation of the cosmic gateway to Eternity.

PHILOSOPHER'S STONE (Illustration by J. A. Knapp, *The Secret Teaching of All Ages* by Manly P. Hall, 1925)

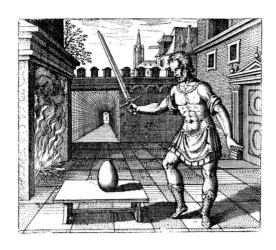

ALCHEMY

It is true without lie, certain and without doubt, that what is below is like what is above, and what is above is like what is below, to accomplish the miracles of the One thing. —The Emerald Tablet of Hermes[1]

ALCHEMY IS KNOWN AS "the Royal Art" (*Ars regia*). The root of the word is the Arabic *al-kimiya,* "black earth," a literal reference to the alluvial mud deposited by the Nile to form the soil of Egypt, and a symbolic reference to the dark First Matter of the Work. Alternatively, the word Alchemy may derive from the Greek *chyma,* "smelting" or "casting."

Alchemy is the precursor of chemistry as well as the repository of the metallurgical wisdom of the ancient world. It encompasses a physical practice. It is also an artisan's craft in which exquisite alloys of metal, dyes, colored glass, and composite materials are developed. In spiritual terms, Alchemy is a symbolic description of the transformation from the dark leaden physicality of earthbound consciousness to the refined gold of the spiritually illuminated being; it maps the inner dynamics that will result in the purification of body, mind, and soul.

Alchemy has existed for thousands of years in cultures as diverse as those of Egypt, Greece, India, China, and the Near East. While there is no single alchemical tradition as such, there is a cross-cultural similarity and cohesiveness to the material. The alchemical tradition that spread throughout Europe and the Near East had its origin within the Egyptian priesthood. The Hermetic philosophy and literature were attributed directly to Hermes Trismegistus, an archetypal figure derived from the Egyptian Thoth, God of Science, measurement, Magick, and writing.

The goal of Alchemy is called the Great Work. It is the purification of the lesser and gross and its elevation to the greater and more refined, whether in metals or in consciousness. The First Matter, *Materia Prima,* is the reduced and original substance and condition of each object of the alchemist's attention. Dark, passive, unformed, virgin, it is the universal field for the imprinting of all forms. Through numerous, time-consuming, and sometimes dangerous processes, the First Matter is transformed into the Philosopher's Stone. This accomplishment is most commonly symbolized by the transformation of lead into gold—the heaviest, darkest, densest, most earthbound, least valuable metal becoming gold: incarnated light; the most glittering, luminous, valuable metal; symbol of the Sun and thereby of spiritual consciousness and attainment.

Alchemical writers were unanimous in preaching and promising the spiritual rewards of the art. Gold as the final goal of the metallic kingdom is a symbol of spiritual illumination, the final goal of human life. In the mineral kingdom, gold represents the perfectly formed offspring of the union of positive and negative, male and female. Gold is the root-essence of lead. It is considered an implicit component of all metals in greater or lesser degree, based on their density, much as the illumined spiritual reality is considered implicit in the soul of each incarnate human, no matter how overlaid with vice and ignorance.

Gold has been recognized for millennia as the most pure metal, a substance of great worth, and a fitting symbol of the sacred. In ancient cultures the priestly class was responsible for the mining, smelting, extraction, and minting of gold. Titus Burckhardt, in his excellent study *Alchemy*, writes that "In archaic cultures . . . seeing everything in relation to the inner unity of man and the cosmos, the preparation of ores is always carried out as a sacred procedure."[2]

Another facet of Alchemy is the search for the Elixir of Life, or Vegetable Stone. Known as the Universal Medicine, its properties include the power to heal the sick, improve health, and prolong life. The search for this panacea ultimately resulted in the discovery of several ingredients now included in the modern pharmacopeia.

Many interpretations have been given to the alchemical allegories. To understand why there are so many different opinions about Alchemy, we must first realize that the body of alchemical literature is enormous. It ranges in content from the ridiculous to the sublime; much of it was intentionally misleading and obscure.

The ratio of "material" to "spiritual" in Alchemy is a major difference of opinion between interpreters of the subject. One school of thought tends to perceive the alchemist as a medieval fool, greedily attempting to enrich himself by turning lead and other base metals to gold. This school, however, also credits Alchemy with giving rise to chemistry and advancing the science and art of metallurgy.

On the other interpretive extreme, the physical and chemical transformation of metals is ignored. Alchemy is perceived as a purely symbolic language for spiritual realities. This school seems to deny much of the written material as well as traditional alchemical legends. For example, Michael Neander in 1586 published in his *Orbis Terrae Partium Succinta Explicato* an account of the great Paracelsus, who heated a pound of mercury in a crucible. When it smoked, he added the Stone of the Philosophers to the crucible. After half an hour, Paracelsus asked what the mixture looked like. Neander replied,

> "It looked yellow, like gold." "Yes," he said, "it is supposed to be gold." I took it out and gold it was. He said, "Take it to the goldsmith who lives above the pharmacy and tell him to pay me for it." I did as he said and the goldsmith weighed it. Its weight was a pound minus half an ounce. And he went for money.[3]

A third school of interpretation asserts that tantric sexuality is the primary underlying reality of alchemical symbolism. It further describes Alchemy as a form of Yoga that includes a doctrine of physical regeneration through the ingestion of various elixirs.

Finally, there is the school of thought that attempts to reduce Alchemy to a fanciful analog of modern psychotherapy, thereby circumscribing it in terms acceptable to secular rationalism.

Alchemy as an oral tradition relied on the apprenticeship of student to master, as well as a lifetime of effort devoted to its practice. Some of the techniques involved in producing the Philosopher's Stone might involve decades of preparation and development.

To best understand Alchemy, the reader ought to consider that there are as many variations in the practice as there are alchemists. There is no canon. One alchemist will see the work as primarily chemical; another, primarily spiritual; and a third will travel the middle ground.

The one indispensable ingredient of the work of Alchemy is prayer. This is what distinguishes Alchemy from a purely physical science. The alchemical prayer may consist of a Divine Name or formula used as a mantra. Through years or decades of this work, some form of success will result. Matter—whether metal, vegetable, or human—will be transformed.

SYMBOLS OF ALCHEMY

The primary symbol of Alchemy is the Philosopher's Stone. This is the highest, most pure perfection of matter, the First Matter elevated to Godhead. The Philosopher's Stone has the power to transform metals and to raise them to its own perfection. Synesios, a 4th century alchemist quoted by Burckhardt, says,

> It is clear what the philosophers mean when they describe the production of our stone as the alteration of natures and the rotation of elements . . . the wet becomes dry, the volatile stable, the spiritual embodied, the fluid solid, water fiery, and the air like earth. Thus all four elements renounce their own nature and, by rotation, transform themselves into one another. . . . Everything comes from One and returns to One.[4]

The means of discovering or "manufacturing" the Philosopher's Stone was concealed in the formula V.I.T.R.I.O.L. *Visita interiora terrae; rectificando invenies occultum lapidem* (Visit the interior of the earth; through purification thou wilt find the hidden stone).

The Four Elements are an important part of Alchemy, as in the other disciplines discussed in this book. The world is seen as consisting of four basic archetypal representations of energy called Fire, Water, Air, and Earth. These are *qualitative states*. A fifth element, Spirit, or *Akasha,* known as the *Quinta essentia* or Quintessence, is conceived as the hub of the wheel of the four elements, all of which participate in its nature. The Four Qualities of *Heat* (Expansion), *Cold* (Contraction), *Humidity* (Dissolution), and *Dryness* (Solidification) mirror the four elements.

The Three Principles of Alchemy are called *Sulphur, Mercury,* and *Salt.* This division is similar to the astrological principles of Cardinal, Mutable, and Fixed and is, once again, a symbolic analog of male, female, and child. Sulphur is active, the Spirit, male, fiery, formative. It produces combustion. It symbolizes the Will and the Word. Mercury is passive, the Soul, female, the menstruum, present in blood and semen. Hindu alchemists call quicksilver the "semen of Shiva," the God of transmutation. It dissolves and produces evaporation. Salt represents the body, which forms a supportive vehicle of incarnation for the spirit. It is static, neutral, the remaining ash that serves to "fix" the volatile spirit.

Alchemy is a correlative of Astrology. Both derive from the Hermetic Tradition. While Astrology studies the heavens, Alchemy studies the earth. The seven holy planets of Astrology are related to the seven holy metals of Alchemy in the following manner:

    Moon = Silver
    Mercury = Mercury (Quicksilver)
    Venus = Copper
    Sun = Gold
    Mars = Iron
    Jupiter = Tin
    Saturn = Lead

The primary operations of metalworking are intrinsic to the language of Alchemy. These include the extraction of pure metal from impure ore through smelting and refining; alloying, or the mixing of two metals together to form a more useful third; and the creation of agents, such as antimony, sulphur, and quicksilver, used for dissolving, purifying, or treating metals to add hardness, fusibility, or color.

Another key to alchemical symbolism is the violence and danger implicit in the extraction of pure metals from the impure ore within which these metals are contained. The resistance of the denser aspects of matter or consciousness to the process of purification can cause poisoning, explosions, or insanity.

The Athanor is the symbol of the human body. The word comes from the Arabic *at-tannur,* meaning "oven," the place where the elixir is prepared. It contains a glass vessel, usually egg-shaped, which symbolizes the undisturbed contemplation. This vessel lies in a sand-bath or ash-pit, symbolically the mastered passions, situated immediately above the fire. Fire and heat are keys in the alchemical process. Heat takes the primary material through its successive stages: solid, liquid, gaseous, and solid again. The heat within the Athanor responsible for the transmutation is threefold: the open heat of the fire (the generative powers), the evenly distributed heat of the ash or sand-bath (the mastered passions of the concentrated mind), and the latent heat of the chemical reaction itself (the vital force). Fire, as a symbol of the generative power aroused and tamed for mystical use, relates Alchemy to Yoga. This fire, stimulated by air passing through holes in the Athanor, either flowing naturally or fanned with bellows, recalls the yogic pranayama breathing techniques used to arouse kundalini.

In the images to follow, we have reproduced the 22 plates of the alchemical masterpiece *Splendor Solis,* along with other visual keys to the alchemical mysteries.

THE 22 ALCHEMICAL STAGES

(Manuscript illuminations, *Splendor Solis*, text by Salomon Trismosin, 1582) This is one of the most famous alchemical manuscripts extant because of the beauty of its plates. All 22 paintings are reproduced here in color. The original manuscript is in the British Museum. There are two current editions of the book in black and white. The Phanes Press edition includes a definitive translation of the text by Joscelyn Godwin. The Yogi Publications edition, edited by Julius Kohn, includes an autobiographical account, written in 1498, of Trismosin's search for, and success with, the Philosopher's Stone.

The pictures and text of *Splendor Solis* clearly identify the alchemical quest as both a spiritual and a physical process. Commentators have noted the intriguing similarity of its images to the 22 Trumps of the Tarot. While the plates may certainly be used as archetypal glyphs for meditation on the process of Initiation, an image-by-image alignment with the Tarot does not seem to exist.

Adam McClean, the editor of the Phanes Press publication, has made an interesting analysis of the pictures, to which the reader is referred. To summarize, he groups the first four plates into the four stages of the *Prima Materia,* or basis of the Work. Next are the seven phases of the *Alchemical Allegory.* The seven plates that follow show the seven stages of *Transformation within the Retort.* He calls the last four plates the four stages of the *End of the Work.* The ultimate goal of the process described in the book is the preparation of the Solar tincture—the Red Stone or Philosopher's Stone—shown in Plate 22, in which the purified Cosmic Sun unites with the fertile Earth and "that which is above unites with that which is below."

In the concluding chapter of the text, Trismosin describes the most precious alchemical art as a gift from God and directs the practitioner to contemplation and meditation in order to understand its processes. In presenting this rarest of manuscripts to the modern world, we can only concur with its venerable author.

1

2

3

4

5

6

7

8

9

10

11

12

13

14

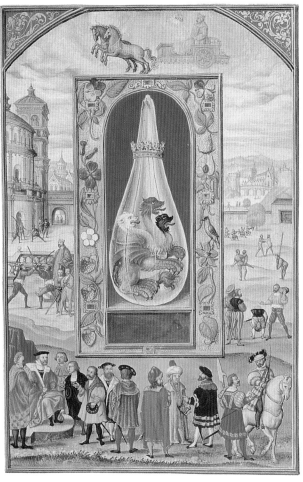

15

16

17

18

19

20

21

22

THE FIRST STAGE OF THE GREAT WORK (Engraving designed by Heinrich Khunrath,
Amphitheater of Eternal Wisdom by Heinrich Khunrath, 1604) Kneeling in a laboratory,
an alchemist prays before a tabernacle inscribed: "Happy the one who follows the advice of
the Lord"; "When we attend strictly to our work God himself will help us." The structure is
reminiscent of the tent of the Israelites in their journey through the desert, symbolizing
the temporary aspect of this part of the work and pointing toward the goal of the more
permanent temple in the distance. The words and images shown in the open books on the
altar symbolize the Wisdom of the Word. The Sanctuary Lamp is the ever-present reality of
God, the Sun and Illuminator. The rising smoke of burning incense indicates the fragrance of
prayer, for only by devotion can the true goal be attained. The inscription over the doorway
at the far end of the hall reads, "While sleeping, watch!"

OUROBOROS (Illustration, *Atalanta Fugiens* by Michael Maier, 1618) The dragon or serpent feeding on its own tail is a symbol of eternity, the cyclic nature of the universe, all-inclusive and all-devouring.

HERMES BIRD (Manuscript illumination, "Riply Scrowle" by James Standysh, 16th century) The alchemical bird is shown consuming its own feathers, preying upon itself like the Ouroboros above. The pelican piercing its own breast to feed its young from its flesh and blood echoes this, as does the mystical Christ, the Dying God whose self-sacrifice brings life to those in His care.

THE MYSTERY OF THE HERMETIC ARTS (Illustration, *Speculum Sophicum Rhodo-Stauroticum* by Theophilus Schweighardt, 1618) In the shrine above is the alchemist at prayer; the lamp illumines the Bible; the incense is the aspiration to the Holy. The laborer at lower left works at normal worldly pursuits, while the alchemist at right is shown in his laboratory. The Virgin of the World stands upon the central pillar of Wisdom with her child, produced by the conjunction of Sun and Moon.

CONSTANT LABOR (Engraving, *A Collection of Emblems Ancient and Moderne* by George Wither, 1635) Wither writes, "Good Hopes, we best accomplish may, by laboring in a constant Way." Here the theme is repeated that the Work is accomplished by Working; in other words, the self-discipline of the Adept is a most important component of the Mystic Path. This message is repeated, in one form or another, through all the world's religious literature.

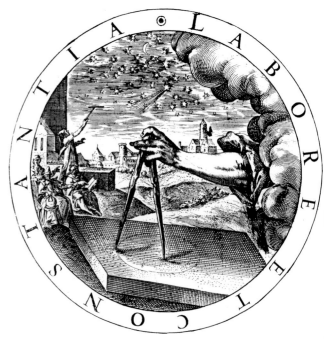

THE HOLY MOUNTAIN OF INITIATION

Engraving by Raphael Custodis, *Cabala, Spiegel der Kunst und Natur* [Cabala, Mirror of Art and Nature] by Steffan Michaelspacher, 1616) The German edition of this work was published the same year as *The Chymical Wedding*. The Latin edition, in 1654, contained a dedication to the Brotherhood of the Rosy Cross. In the center of the Mountain is the Royal Bridal Chamber, in which sit the King and Queen. Upon the roof are emblems of the Sun and Moon; the Phoenix rises in triumph. Along the Mountain are the seven planets, around which are the Zodiac and the four Elements. The steps leading to the Chamber show the alchemical stages of the Work. The alchemist approaches blindfolded. The rabbits suggest that awareness of the Secret is concealed within the intuitive nature.

THE REIGN OF THE WISE (Engraving, *A Collection of Emblems Ancient and Moderne* by George Wither, 1635) Wither writes, "He, over the Stars doth reign, that unto Wisdom can attain." Now the Great Work is complete and the promised mastery is reached. For "The Soul of Man is nobler than the Spheres . . . the Lord of all that God hath made." The Adept has internalized the Divine within himself, demonstrated by the emblem of the All-Seeing Eye upon his heart.

THOTH OF THE FOUR WINDS (*Papyrus of Hor,* Ptlomaic Period, ca. 300 B.C.E., Egypt)

TAROT

As an erudite Kabbalistic book, all combinations of which reveal the harmonies preexisting between signs, letters and numbers, the practical value of the Tarot is truly and above all marvelous. A prisoner devoid of books, had he only a Tarot of which he knew how to make use, could in a few years acquire a universal science, and converse with an unequalled doctrine and inexhaustible eloquence. —Transcendental Magic *by Éliphas Lévi[1]*

IN 1781, COURT DE GEBELIN, in his *Monde Primitif*, called the Tarot the *Book of Thoth*, in honor of the Egyptian god of Magick and Divination. With the Tarot, the theory of correspondence reaches its highest pitch. The properly prepared aspirant approaches the universe with the request that light be shed on a certain subject and that true insights be derived from the apparently random patterns made by a series of archetypal images.

Implicit in divination is a belief in Higher Consciousness directing the process. This is true even if the Higher Consciousness is defined merely as the subconscious mind of the diviner.

The Tarot is a resume of the entire spectrum of the Mystery Traditions. It is composed of the primary symbols of Astrology. It hints at the truths concealed in Alchemy. Tarot meditation—in which the cards function as energy doorways for the focusing of concentration—makes use of the techniques of Magick. In its structure, the Tarot is a schematic representation of the Kabbalistic Tree of Life. Its images depict the psychospiritual processes of the Initiatic Journey.

The cards first appeared in the 14th century. One of the mythical histories of the origins of Tarot places its development around the year 1200. After the destruction of the Alexandrian library in the 4th century, Initiates from many different lands and language groups agreed to meet periodically. They chose to hold council in Fez, Morocco—at that time the literary and scientific capital of the world. Here they determined to enshrine the Secret Teaching in as universal a fashion as possible. They chose the form of pictures, linked by the science of numbers, that could be read by those who did not share a common language. They determined that the best way to guard and keep secret the Mysteries was to "profane" them—that is, to disguise the Wisdom Teachings of the ages as an ordinary pack of playing cards, which could be used for both divination and gambling. They also decided to pass these cards, and some of the secrets of their use in divination, to the nomadic gypsies. These wanderers would cross and recross the known world bringing the cards with them, thus preserving the hidden knowledge.

Like the Kabbalah discussed in chapter 2, the Tarot is divided in groups of four, ten, and 22. There are four Suits, within each of which are ten small cards numbered ace through ten. These 40 small cards are called the Minor Arcana, or Lesser Mysteries. Each suit also has four Court Cards, numbering in total 16. Finally, there are 22 Trumps, or Major Arcana—Greater Mysteries—corresponding to the letters of the Hebrew Alphabet.

Following are brief descriptions of the meanings of the cards, divided by group. It will be helpful to refer to the chapter on Kabbalah and to the Tree of Life diagram on page 29 during the following discussion. The mystical Golden Dawn titles of the Tarot cards are presented to give the reader a sense of the deeper esoteric significance of the cards and to suggest a direction for meditation. These names are derived from *Book T*, the secret Golden Dawn instruction on Tarot written by S. L. MacGregor Mathers. The Suggested Reading List includes useful books for further study.

THE FOUR SUITS

(Element, Magick Power, Part of Self, Area of Life)

WANDS: Fire, To Will, the Will, Career, goals, energy
CUPS: Water, To Know, the Emotions, Love, family, pleasure
SWORDS: Air, To Dare, the Mind, Ideas, challenges, troubles
DISKS: Earth, To Keep Silence, the Body, Finances, material matters

THE COURT CARDS

KNIGHT (KING) OF WANDS: The Lord of the Flame and Lightning; the King of the Spirits of Fire
KNIGHT OF CUPS: The Lord of the Waves and the Waters; the King of the Hosts of the Sea
KNIGHT OF SWORDS: The Lord of the Wind and the Breezes; the King of the Spirits of Air
KNIGHT OF DISKS: The Lord of the Wide and Fertile Land; the King of the Spirits of Earth

QUEEN OF WANDS: The Queen of the Thrones of Flame
QUEEN OF CUPS: The Queen of the Thrones of the Waters

QUEEN OF SWORDS: The Queen of the Thrones of Air
QUEEN OF DISKS: The Queen of the Thrones of Earth

PRINCE (KNIGHT) OF WANDS: The Prince of the Chariot of Fire
PRINCE OF CUPS: The Prince of the Chariot of the Waters
PRINCE OF SWORDS: The Prince of the Chariot of Air
PRINCE OF DISKS: The Prince of the Chariot of Earth

PRINCESS (PAGE) OF WANDS: The Princess of the Shining Flame; the Rose of the Palace of Fire
PRINCESS OF CUPS: The Princess of the Waters; the Lotus of the Palace of the Floods
PRINCESS OF SWORDS: The Princess of the Rushing Winds; the Lotus of the Palace of Air
PRINCESS OF DISKS: The Princess of the Echoing Hills; the Rose of the Palace of Earth

THE MINOR ARCANA (Sephira and its Meaning)

ACES: *Kether*, Original elemental force in its purest, unadulterated form.
WANDS: The Root of the Powers of Fire
CUPS: The Root of the Powers of Water
SWORDS: The Root of the Powers of Air
DISKS: The Root of the Powers of Earth

TWOS: *Chokmah*, Original harmonious condition in the idea of the Element.
| WANDS: Dominion | CUPS: Love |
| SWORDS: Peace Restored | DISKS: Harmonious Change |

THREES: *Binah*, Fertilization and stabilization of the Element.
| WANDS: Established Strength | CUPS: Abundance |
| SWORDS: Sorrow | DISKS: Material Works |

FOURS: *Chesed*, Solidification and materialization of the Element, the Rule of Law.
| WANDS: Perfected Work | CUPS: Pleasure |
| SWORDS: Rest from Strife | DISKS: Earthly Power |

FIVES: *Geburah*, Storm and stress, motion, and disturbance within the Element.
| WANDS: Strife | CUPS: Loss in Pleasure |
| SWORDS: Defeat | DISKS: Material Trouble |

SIXES: *Tiphareth*, Balance, harmonization, beauty in the form of the Element.
| WANDS: Victory | CUPS: Pleasure |
| SWORDS: Earned Success | DISKS: Material Success |

SEVENS: *Netzach*, Struggle and weakness, lack of balance, the degeneration of the Element.
| WANDS: Valor (implies fear) | CUPS: Illusionary Success |
| SWORDS: Unstable Effort | DISKS: Success Unfulfilled |

EIGHTS: *Hod*, Same inherent defects as the Sevens, because they are off the Middle Pillar and low down on the Tree of Life; however, there is a slight remedy, and Eight is a stronger and more fortunate expression of the Element.
| WANDS: Swiftness | CUPS: Abandoned Success |
| SWORDS: Shortened Force | DISKS: Prudence |

NINES: *Yesod*, Crystallization of energy of the Element, full impact of the elemental force in a material sense.

WANDS: Great Strength CUPS: Material Happiness
SWORDS: Despair and Cruelty DISKS: Material Gain

TENS: *Malkuth*, The Elements, within Matter, without elasticity, the end of the process of emanation, finality.

WANDS: Oppression CUPS: Perfected Success
SWORDS: Ruin DISKS: Wealth

THE MAJOR ARCANA (Hebrew Letter, English Meaning, Attribution of *Sepher Yetzirah*). Note: The *Sepher Yetzirah*, an early Kabbalistic text discussed in chapter 2, assigns elements, planets, and signs to each letter. Also, the traditional Kabbalistic analysis of the Letters ascribes importance to each aspect of the Letter, including its shape, said to conceal hidden meaning; numeration; and literal meaning, given in parentheses in the list below. As an example of the symbolic importance of the meaning of a Letter, *Daleth* means "Door." It is assigned by the *Sepher Yetzirah* to the planet Venus, a symbol of the Goddess, who is the "doorway of life" through birth and the "doorway to eternity" through the return to Her womb in death. Finally, the number of the Tarot Trump given below is not the numeric value of the Hebrew letter.

0. THE FOOL: *Aleph* (Ox), Air, The Spirit of the Aether
I. THE MAGICIAN: *Beth* (House), Mercury, The Magus of Power
II. THE HIGH PRIESTESS: *Gimel* (Camel), Moon, The Priestess of the Silver Star
III. THE EMPRESS: *Daleth* (Door), Venus, The Daughter of the Mighty Ones
IV. THE EMPEROR: *Tzaddi* (Fish Hook), Aries, The Sun of the Morning, Chief among the Mighty
V. THE HIEROPHANT: *Vav* (Nail), Taurus, The Magus of the Eternal
VI. THE LOVERS: *Zain* (Sword), Gemini, The Children of the Voice, the Oracles of the Mighty Gods
VII. THE CHARIOT: *Cheth* (Fence), Cancer, The Child of the Powers of the Waters; the Lord of the Triumph of Light
VIII. ADJUSTMENT (JUSTICE): *Lamed* (Ox Goad), Libra, The Daughter of the Lords of Truth, the Ruler of the Balance
IX. THE HERMIT: *Yod* (Hand), Virgo, The Magus of the Voice of Power, the Prophet of the Eternal
X. THE WHEEL OF FORTUNE: *Kaph* (Palm), Jupiter, The Lord of the Forces of Life
XI. LUST (STRENGTH, FORTITUDE): *Teth* (Serpent), Leo, The Daughter of the Flaming Sword
XII. THE HANGED MAN: *Mem* (Water), Water, The Spirit of the Mighty Waters
XIII. DEATH: *Nun* (Fish), Scorpio, The Child of the Great Transformers, the Lord of the Gates of Death

XIV. ART (TEMPERANCE): *Samekh* (Prop), Sagittarius, The Daughter of the Reconcilers, the Bringer-Forth of Life
XV. THE DEVIL: *Ayin* (Eye), Capricorn, The Lord of the Gates of Matter, the Child of the Forces of Time
XVI. THE TOWER: *Peh* (Mouth), Mars, The Lord of the Hosts of the Mighty
XVII. THE STAR: *Heh* (Window), Aquarius, The Daughter of the Firmament, the Dweller between the Waters
XVIII. THE MOON: *Qoph* (Back of Head), Pisces, The Ruler of Flux and Reflux, the Child of the Sons of the Mighty
XIX. THE SUN: *Resh* (Head), Sun, The Lord of the Fire of the World
XX. THE AEON (JUDGMENT): *Shin* (Tooth), Fire, The Spirit of the Primal Fire
XXI. THE UNIVERSE (THE WORLD): *Tau* (Cross), Saturn, The Great One of the Night of Time

The Tree of Life may be used for the interpretation of the cards. For example, each of the 40 small cards is assigned to one of the ten Sephiroth and is modified by the elementary attribution of its Suit. Thus, all cards numbered 5 will imply some kind of disrupting influence, as the number 5 is related to Motion (see the Kabbalah chapter). The number 5 is also assigned to the Sphere of Mars (see the diagram on page 29), whose energy is bold and aggressive, as discussed in the Astrology chapter. Now, this combination of energies bodes ill in the suit of Cups (Water), as it conflicts with the flowing and passive nature of that element. However, in the highly active suit of Wands (Fire) the combination of energies represented by the number 5 is more at home.

The few attributions and cross-references included here for the cards should clarify the assertion that the Tarot recapitulates the entire Western Esoteric Tradition. Its value as a pictorial symbol reference for study and meditation is incalculable. More than any other of the disciplines mentioned in this book, the Tarot is an actual symbolic language. When used appropriately, the *Book of Thoth* is a true guide to the Mysteries, as well as a remarkably useful tool for divination.

In the images to follow, we include the Major Arcana from four decks whose design we feel is seminal to the study of the development of the Tarot: The Visconti Tarot, the earliest medieval example; the Marseilles deck, the traditional deck from which all later decks have been derived; the Waite deck, the most popular and therefore the most influential in preserving the cards in general usage; and the Crowley deck, the most comprehensive development of the Tarot symbols to date.

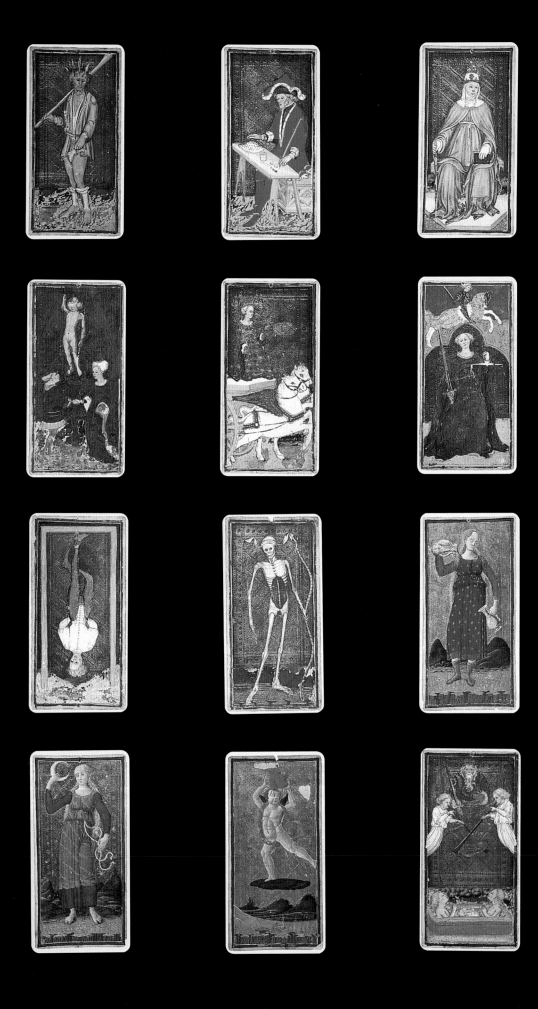

VISCONTI DECK This Italian deck dates to about 1450 and is the earliest most complete Tarot deck. It is missing four cards. Two of the Trumps, —the Devil (card 15) and the Tower (card 16)—shown above are modern interpretations, commissioned by the publisher of the deck, U.S. Games. The original cards are both untitled and unnumbered. The sequence presented here is the traditional sequence, which dates to 1556 or 1557, the earliest known printed deck with numbers on the Major Arcana.

THE FOOL

THE MAGICIAN

THE HIGH PRIESTESS

THE LOVER

THE CHARIOT

JUSTICE

THE HANGED MAN

DEATH

TEMPERANCE

THE MOON

THE SUN

JUDGEMENT

THE EMPRESS

THE EMPEROR

THE POPE

THE HERMIT

THE WHEEL OF FORTUNE

FORCE

THE DEVIL

THE TOWER OF DESTRUCTION

THE STAR

THE WORLD

MARSEILLES DECK This French deck is the earliest Tarot deck to achieve widespread fame and prominence. It appeared in 1748 and thereby recorded the tradition that had by then become established regarding the images and the sequence of the Major Arcana of the Tarot. This deck also passed along these attributions to later designers and writers. The unnumbered Fool card was often placed between the Sun and Judgment; however, here it is located at the zero position preceding one.

THE FOOL.

THE MAGICIAN.

THE HIGH PRIESTESS

THE LOVERS.

THE CHARIOT.

STRENGTH.

THE HANGED MAN.

DEATH.

TEMPERANCE.

THE MOON.

THE SUN.

JUDGEMENT.

THE EMPRESS.

THE EMPEROR.

THE HIEROPHANT

THE HERMIT.

WHEEL of FORTUNE.

JUSTICE.

THE DEVIL.

THE TOWER.

THE STAR.

THE WORLD.

WAITE DECK This is the most popular modern Tarot deck, dating from 1910. Waite deliberately obscured the symbolism of the Golden Dawn, from whom he learned Tarot. He also revised the traditional order of the cards to reflect the astrological sequence of the signs. Leo—Strength (card 8)—changes place in this deck with Libra—Justice (card 11). Paul Foster Case followed Waite's revision brilliantly. His attributions of Trump number and Sign of the Zodiac to the cards establish the symbolic geometry of a circle for the Major Arcana. See his important work *Tarot: A Key to the Wisdom of the Ages* for a detailed discussion.

0   The Fool

I   The Magus

II   The Priestess

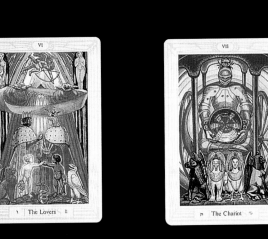

VI   The Lovers

VII   The Chariot

VIII   Adjustment

XII   The Hanged Man

XIII   Death

XIV   Art

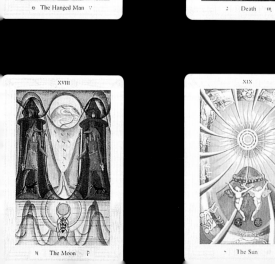

XVIII   The Moon

XIX   The Sun

XX   The Aeon

III   The Empress

IV   The Emperor

V   The Hierophant

IX   The Hermit

X   Fortune

XI   Lust

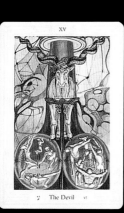

XV   The Devil

XVI   The Tower

XVII   The Star

XXI   The Universe

CROWLEY DECK This most interesting development of the Tarot was published in 1944. Crowley returned to the traditional sequence, established centuries earlier, in which Libra (card 8) and Leo (card 11) are out of their normal astrological order. Crowley, however, also reassigned the zodiacal attributions of the Emperor—Aquarius (card 4)—and the Star—Aries (card 17). He did this while maintaining their traditional numerical sequence. This perfectly balances the attributions of the Tarot for the first time in history. The symbolic geometry of the Major Arcana now becomes that of the Mobius strip. Please see Crowley's *The Book of Thoth* for clarification of this revolutionary discovery.

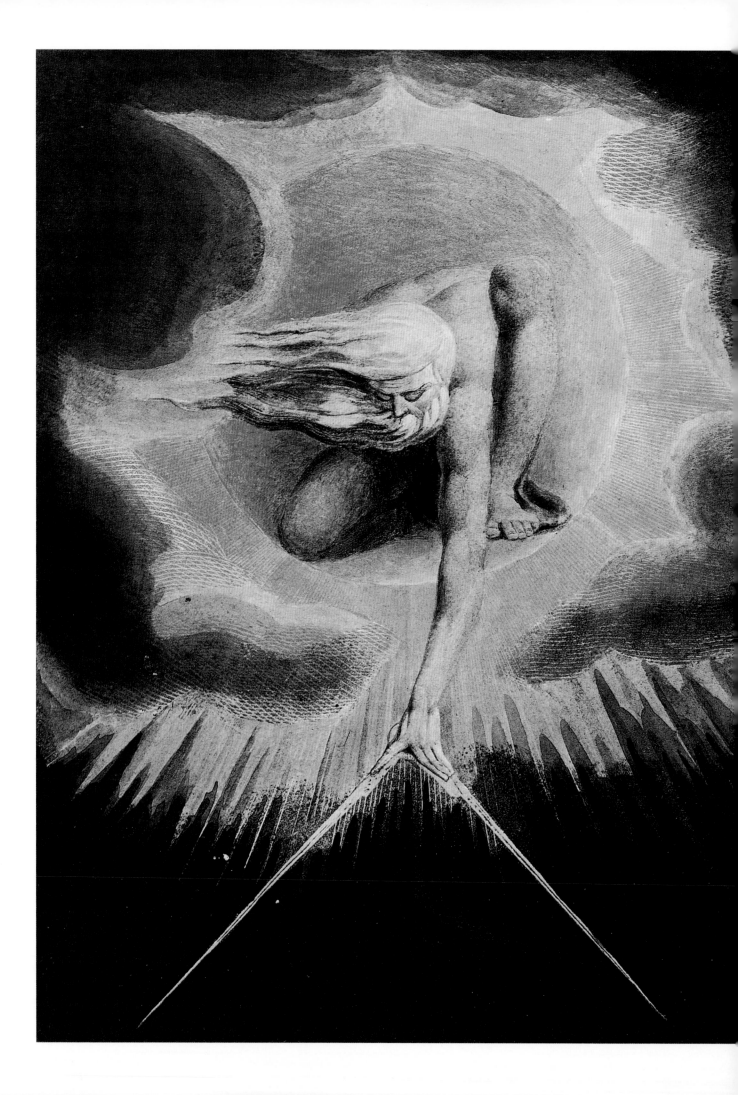

SYMBOLIST
AND VISIONARY ART

BY SEAN KONECKY

AS WE HAVE SEEN THROUGHOUT THE PRESENT WORK, the symbolic vocabulary through which the Esoteric Tradition has been conveyed has had a great influence on, and in turn has been greatly influenced by, a lineage of artists. This line runs from antiquity through the anonymous masters of the Middle Ages, the great painters of the Renaissance, and the 19th century Symbolists to artists of the present day. Edgar Wind, in his important study of Renaissance art,[1] demonstrates the debt that Botticelli, Titian, and Michelangelo, among others, owed to the Neoplatonist philosophies of their contemporaries Marselio Ficino and Pico della Mirandola. Their paintings, symbolic tableaux to be read by Initiates, elaborated these hidden ideas and gave them form.

The Romantic Revolution, with its exaltation of the irrational, along with an exhaustion of academic approaches to art, fostered a keen receptivity to occult ideas in the late 19th century. An impatient desire for a complete rupture with the existing models and procedures of painting led to the formation of the Pre-Raphaelite Movement in 1850. Its founders, Rosetti, Hunt, and Millais, wanted to return to what they saw as the uncorrupted painting of the Middle

OPPOSITE: **THE ANCIENT OF DAYS** (Illustration by William Blake for his poetic work "Europe," 1794) Both poet and artist, Blake illustrated his own poetic work. He also labored to create his own cosmology and mythology, based upon his readings of the Bible, the teachings of Swedenborg, and his own besetting visions. According to his early biographer, Gilchrist, Blake had his first vision at the age of eight or ten of "a tree filled with angels." This illustration suggests a gnostic approach to the Creator as a lesser, fallible God. For Blake, Creation signaled a fall from a heavenly state, followed by a redemption through the powers of the imagination. Blake's influence was of immeasurable importance to the later Pre-Raphaelite and Symbolist movements.

Ages and the Quattrocento, and that entailed a concern for and comfort with the symbol and its capacity to point from the visible to the invisible. Their fanatic loyalty to the faithful transcription of the apparent is their fundamental shortcoming. One might say that they were so overcome and seduced by the appearance of the symbol that they looked no further.

The Symbolist school that succeeded them sought to develop a stereoscopic perspective. The agenda was set by Gustav Moreau, whose paintings intoxicate the viewer with the evocative richness of the symbol while pointing toward a veiled reality. He provided the critical momentum for a movement that was to include such diverse figures as Gauguin, Serusier, and Ransom; Bocklin, Ensor, and Khnoppf; and Redon, and later Kandinsky. For them, the theory of correspondences was filtered through the poetics and criticism of Baudelaire. His poem "Correspondances" begins:

La nature est un temple ou de vivants piliers
Laissent parfois sortir de confuses paroles
L'homme y passe a travers des forets de symboles
Qui l'observent avec des regards fanmiliers.

(Nature is a temple whose living columns sometimes yield confusing messages; man passes there across a forest of a symbols which cast their familiar glances at him.)[2]

At the same time the impact of Hermetic ideas was making itself felt through the agency of Huysmans, whose *A Rebours* was tantamount to a manifesto for this generation, and through Sar Peladan and his exhibitions at the Salon de la Rose + Croix. Paul Serusier, a widely read disciple of Gauguin, painted *The Talisman* and electrified a new group of painters who called themselves *Nabis* (in Hebrew, "Prophets"). They testified that every emotion and every sensation had an equivalent or correspondent color.

The achievement of the Symbolists was until recently discounted. Paradoxically it was Maurice Denis, one of the key practitioners of the Symbolist school, who pointed toward the new direction in art, one that would lead away from the symbol: "Remember that a picture . . . is essentially a flat surface covered with colors assembled in a certain order."[3] The programmatic enactment of this dictum occupied art and art criticism for the first half of the 20th century. Iconography persisted in an ambiguous way in the works of Surrealism before finding its way back into the artistic mainstream, as in the works of such artists as Anselm Kiefer and Francesco Clemente.

Another approach to art, visionary rather than symbolic, in some ways exceeds the Symbolist aesthetic. Here art becomes the literal description of extreme psychological states. The immediacy of work of this kind can be found in many naive painters, and especially in works of those commonly labeled insane. This area is just beginning to gain attention.

This same immediacy is also encountered in the work of those rare individuals in whom the gift or curse of transcendent vision is coupled with a fully developed artistic sensibility. Their dual allegiance—to the exigencies of their art and to their experience—is a particularly heavy burden. Blake and Van Gogh are perhaps the two most familiar exemplars of this demanding form of the artistic enterprise.

Practicing art of this kind is a balancing act. The artist fundamentally is committed to the sensory world; color, line, and form are the flesh and sinews of his work. The mystic follows the words of Plotinus and has to press "onwards to the inmost sanctuary, leaving behind the statues in the outer temple."[4] Perhaps Redon, with whose *Silence* we conclude this work, offers us the most profound harmonies. His work is Beauty. While the artist may beckon us further, ultimately he must remain silent.

PRIMAVERA (Painting by Sandro Botticelli, ca. 1478) Botticelli's painting is universally known, but its iconographic significance has been just as widely misinterpreted. *In Pagan Mysteries and the Renaissance,* Edgar Warren Wind traces the impact of the Neoplatonic philosophy of Marselio Ficino and Pico della Mirandola on the major artistic figures of the period and reveals the *Primavera* as a profound meditation on the Neoplatonic doctrine of love. The central figure is Venus, whose movement into manifestation is threefold. Thus, to her left is a dynamic triad of figures representing the initiation into love. To her right the three Graces are engaged in love's harmonious dance. Mercury stands apart at the far left to suggest, perhaps, an aspect of love that is never fully drawn into the world of appearances. This work of Botticelli aptly demonstrates the allegorical method: The beauty of the work is clear to the most casual viewer, but a deeper level of intent surrenders itself to the initiate.

OVERLEAF LEFT: THE APPARITION (Painting by Gustave Moreau, 1875) Moreau is the central figure in the Symbolist movement. His art blends elements of Italian Renaissance painting with an exoticism that came from his study of Indian art and thought. He conceived his works as elaborate allegories tracing the development of the soul; but the dominating impression they leave is of an overwhelming languor, a staggering abundance of imagery that leads finally to satiety. Underlying all of his major painting is the fear of self-abandonment in the voluptuous. Unmistakable sexual fears dominate *The Apparition,* in which the severed head of John the Baptist appears to Salome. Here, as throughout Moreau's work, the double-faced nature of the symbol interweaves the spiritual and the sexual with extreme suggestiveness.

OVERLEAF RIGHT: MOTHER OF THE WORLD (Painting by Nicholas Roerich, n.d.) Roerich's work is an expression of an extraordinary life. He is best known for his designs of the sets and costumes for Diaghilev's original performance of Stravinsky's *Rites of Spring.* His art unites Eastern and Western traditions of spirituality. *Mother of the World* exemplifies this synthetic approach. The Marian figure at the center of the canvas is surrounded by celestial Bodhisattvas. Kneeling to her right is a nun, and to her left is an Eastern spiritual aspirant. In his own words, "To both East and West, the image of the Great Mother—womanhood—is the bridge of ultimate unification."

THE WINGED HORSE (Watercolor by George Russell [A.E.], ca. 1910) A.E. was both artist and poet. His close friend W. B. Yeats spoke at length about him in his autobiographical writings. They first met at art school. Yeats, struck by the effortless manner with which A.E. worked, observed that "he did not want to paint the model as we tried to for some other image rose always before his eyes." Later in his *Dramatis Personae* Yeats reports that "it was known that he [A.E.] sees visions continually." The two disagreed about the artistic use to which these visions should be put. "He and I often quarreled. . . . I thought symbolic what he thought real like the man and woman who passed him by on the road." This points to A.E.'s strengths and weaknesses as an artist. His finest works, such as *The Winged Horse,* have the trembling evanescence of a vision just glimpsed, but they are not subjected to the deepest scrutiny. Beautifully suggestive yet ephemeral, his painting pales in comparison with Blake's visionary transcriptions, into which are poured the full concentration of the artistic imagination.

OPPOSITE ABOVE: DANTE DRAWING AN ANGEL ON THE ANNIVERSARY OF BEATRICE'S DEATH (Painting by Dante Gabriel Rossetti, ca. 1860) On January 1, 1850, a new magazine entitled *The Germ* appeared in London. It announced the formation of the Pre-Raphaelite Brotherhood. Rossetti, William Holman Hunt, and John Everett Millais adopted the form of a secret society to enact what they thought would be a purification of the stale artistic conventions of the period. Their return to medieval and early Renaissance models opened the door to mythic patterns and symbolism that had been largely forgotten.

OPPOSITE BELOW: THE ISLAND OF THE DEAD (Painting by Arnold Bocklin, 1880) Arnold Bocklin was the major Swiss exponent of the Symbolist style, which was launched in Paris by Gustave Moreau. He infused his canvases with a distinct sense of the uncanny. He was fascinated by thresholds and boundaries, as can be seen in his paintings of mermaids and centaurs, and by journeys to unknown worlds, as in *The Island of the Dead.* This unsettling painting was given its present title by an art dealer. Bocklin called it simply "a picture for dreaming over," leaving the viewer with the burden of interpretation.

OLIVE TREES (Painting by Vincent Van Gogh, 1889) Van Gogh may seem somewhat out of place in the present work. He was not a student of the occult, nor did he employ the symbolic vocabulary that we explore here; his approach was different. He sublimated his passionate religious convictions in his art. Painting became for him a sustaining religion. His late work, primarily landscapes, like the one presented here, lays bare the burning energy at the heart of matter. This work was completed during periods of lucidity that alternated with episodes of the madness that proved to be his undoing.

OPPOSITE: HOLY FIRE (Painting by Alex Gray, left panel of triptych) This contemporary painter is an heir to the Symbolist tradition. His work points to an idea world, but one, unlike that of the Symbolists, unencumbered by repressed unconscious elements. His painting makes the human figure central, as does Blake's, and then grounds it with the precision of medical drawing to create studies in spiritual anatomy. *The Holy Fire* triptych depicts three stages: the seeker penetrated by the Spirit, his self-annihilation in union with the Absolute, and his return as an Enlightened Being to the world. The first stage, shown here, wrenchingly portrays the consciousness of separateness and the impact of the Divine on the frame of the human personality.

SILENCE (Painting by Odilon Redon, ca. 1911) Redon here presents us with a portrait of Harpocrates, the God of Mystical Silence, whose characteristic gesture is the forefinger pressed before his lips. This gesture was later transferred to Hermes the Mystagogue, who guides souls out of Multiplicity. Ultimately, the greatest mystery cannot be seen or spoken; it is beyond the grasp of the intellect and all symbolic representation.

Notes to the Text

INTRODUCTION

1 Burckhardt, *Alchemy*, London, Stuart & Watkins, 1967, p. 11.
2 Quoted in Yates, *Giordano Bruno and the Hermetic Tradition*, Chicago, University of Chicago, 1991, p. 37.
3 Goelet (ed.), *The Egyptian Book of the Dead, The Book of Going Forth by Day*, San Francisico, Chronicle Books, 1994, 1998.

KABBALAH AND THE TREE OF LIFE

1 Ginsberg, *The Collected Poems of Allen Ginsberg 1947–1980*, New York, Harper & Row, 1984, p. 127.
2 Kaplan, *Sefer Yetzirah*, York Beach, ME, Weiser, 1990, p. xiv.
3 Crowley, *The Book of Thoth*, York Beach, ME, Weiser, 1969, p. 13.

INITIATION

1 Crowley, *Equinox of the Gods*, Scottsdale, New Falcon, 1991, p. 79.
2 Taylor (trans.), *Iamblichus On the Mysteries*, London, Stuart & Watkins, 1968, p. 23.
3 Ibid., p. 55.
4 Singh, *The Persian Mystics, The Invocations of Abdullah Ansari*, London, John Murray, 1951, p. 38.
5 Crowley, *The Magical Diaries of Aleister Crowley 1923*, (ed. Stephen Skinner), New York, Samuel Weiser, 1979, p. 21.
6 *Iamblichus On the Mysteries*, p. 272.
7 Donne, "Holy Sonnet, X" in *The Literature of Renaissance England*, ed. Hollander and Kermode, New York, Oxford Univ. Press, 1973, p. 552.
8 Eschenbach, *Parzival*, New York, Vintage, 1961.
9 Matarasso, *Quest of the Holy Grail*, Baltimore, Penguin, 1975, p. 20.

MAGICK AND THE GODS

1 Quoted in *Giordano Bruno and the Hermetic Tradition*, p. 32.
2 Crowley, *Magick in Theory and Practice*, New York, Magickal Childe, p. xii.
3 *King James Bible*, Camden, Thomas Nelson, 1970, p. 84.
4 *Magick in Theory and Practice*, p. xiii.
5 Crowley (ed.), *The Goetia*, London, The Equinox, 1976, p. 6.
6 Burroughs, Review of *The Necronomicon*, Letter, April 7, 1978.

SECRET SOCIETIES

1 *Zanoni*, Sir Edward Bulwer Lytton, Philadelphia, J. B. Lippincott & Co., 1884, vol. I, pp. 140–41.
2 Crowley, *The Holy Books of Thelema*, York Beach, ME, Weiser, 1988, p. xxxix.
3 Fortune, *The Esoteric Orders and their Work*, St. Paul, Llewelyn Publications, 1971, p. 97.
4 Ibid., p. 37
5 *Zanoni*, vol. II, p. 50.

SEXUALITY

1 *King James Bible*, p. 562.
2 *The Holy Books of Thelema*, p. 109.
3 Blake, *The Marriage of Heaven and Hell*, New York, Oxford University Press, 1975, p. xxii.
4 *The Holy Books of Thelema*, p. 112.
5 See, Wind, *Pagan Mysteries in the Renaissance*, London, Faber and Faber, 1958, chapter 10.
6 *The Persian Mystics*, p. 30.
7 Mathers, *The Sacred Magic of Abramelin*, Chicago, de Laurence, 1948, p. 81.
8 *The Holy Books of Thelema*, p. 208.
9 Ibid., p. 107.

ALCHEMY

1 Klossowski de Rola, *Alchemy: The Secret Art*, New York, Avon, 1973, p. 15.
2 Burckhardt, *Alchemy*, p. 12.
3 Cavendish, *Man, Myth and Magic*, New York, Marshall Cavendish, p. 52.
4 Burckhardt, *Alchemy*, p. 96.

TAROT

1 Lévi, *Transcendental Magic*, York Beach, ME, Weiser, 1991, p. 394.

SYMBOLIST AND VISIONARY ART

1 *Pagan Mysteries in the Renaissance*.
2 Baudelaire, *Les Fleurs du Mal et Autre Poémes*, Paris, Garnier-Flammarion, 1964, p. 39.
3 Quoted in Cogeval, *Post-Impressionists*, Secaucus, NJ, Wellfleet Press, 1988, p. 90.
4 Quoted in *Pagan Mysteries in the Renaissance*, p. 12.

SUGGESTED READING LIST

In many cases, books listed under one heading could be put in numerous other categories, and where this is true, the titles have been marked with an asterisk. Initiation has the most references because its truth spreads throughout all cultures and religions. Initiation is, in fact, the point of it all.

ASTROLOGY AND COSMOLOGY

The Astrologer's Handbook, Sakoian & Acker (Harper & Row)

Astrology, Ronald C. Davison (Arco Books)

Astrology: The Celestial Mirror, Warren Kenton (Avon)

Astrology: History, Symbols and Signs, Solange de Maily Nesle (Inner Traditions)

*Ancient Jewish Art, Gabrielle Sed-Rajna (Chartwell Books)

The General Principles of Astrology, Aleister Crowley (Weiser)

KABBALAH AND THE TREE OF LIFE

The Anatomy of the Body of God, Frater Achad (Weiser)

*The Bible, King James edition

Collected Poems, Allen Ginsberg (Harper & Row)

A Garden of Pomegranates, Israel Regardie (Llewellyn)

*The Egyptian Book of the Dead: The Book of Going Forth by Day, Goelet (ed.) (Chronicle Books)

*The Hidden Lore, Kenneth and Steffi Grant (Skoob Books)

Italian Renaissance Illuminations, J. J. G. Alexander (Braziller)

Jewish Life in the Middle Ages, Metzger (Chartwell Books)

The Kabbalah Unveiled, S. L. MacGregor Mathers (Weiser)

Meditation and Kabbalah, Aryeh Kaplan (Weiser)

*The Middle Pillar, Israel Regardie (Llewlyn)

The Mystical Qabalah, Dion Fortune (Weiser)

A Practical Guide to Qabalistic Symbolism, Gareth Knight (Weiser)

Sefer Yetzirah, Aryeh Kaplan (Weiser)

777, Aleister Crowley (Weiser)

*The Tree of Life, Israel Regardie (Weiser)

The Tree of Life: Image of the Cosmos, Roger Cook (Avon)

The Zohar, Sperling & Simon (trans.) (Soncino Press)

INITIATION

Bhagavad Gita, Johnston (trans.) (Watkins)

Black Elk Speaks, Neihardt (Univ. of Nebraska Press)

The Book of the Law, Aleister Crowley (Weiser)

Captain Sir Richard Francis Burton, Edward Rice (Scribner)

Chakras, Harish Johari (Destiny Books)

A Christian Rosencreutz Anthology, Paul M. Allen (Rudolf Steiner Publications)

Codex Rosae Crucis, Manly Hall (Philosophical Research Society)

Chaldean Oracles of Julianus, Westcott (ed.) (Heptangle Books)

Dhammapadha, P. Lal (trans.) (Noonday Press)

The Epic of Gilgamesh (Penguin Books)

From Ritual to Romance, Jesse L. Weston (Anchor)

Gods of the Egyptians, E. A. Wallis Budge (Methuen)

Golden Bough, Sir James G. Frazer (Macmillan & Company)

The Golden Verses of Pythagoras, Fabre d'Olivet (Weiser)

The Grail: Quest for the Eternal, John Matthews (Avon)

Her Bak, Isha Schwaller De Lubicz (Inner Traditions)

The Hero with a Thousand Faces, Joseph Campbell (Princeton University Press)

The Hindu Pantheon, Moor (Philosophical Research Society)

The Holy Books of Thelema, Aleister Crowley (Weiser)

The Hundred Tales of Wisdom, Idries Shah
  (Octagon Press)
The I Ching, Wilhelm/Baynes (trans.) (Princeton
  Univ. Press)
Iamblichus on the Mysteries, Thomas Taylor
  (trans.) (Watkins)
Inanna, Wolkstein & Kramer (Harper Collins)
Initiation, Elisabeth Haich (Allen and Unwin)
The Kybalion, Three Initiates (Yogi Publication
  Society)
Le Morte D'Arthur, Sir Thomas Mallory (University
  Books)
The Library by Apollodorus, Frazer (trans.) (Loeb
  Library)
Life of Apollonius by Philostratus, Conybeare
  (trans.) (Loeb Library)
Life of Pythagoras, Iamblichus, Thomas Taylor
  (trans.) (Inner Traditions)
Light on the Path, Mabel Collins (Quest Books)
*Meditation Symbols in Eastern and Western
  Mysteries*, Manly P. Hall, (Philosophical Research
  Society)
Monuments of Egypt, (Princeton Architectural
  Press)
Mystical Hymns of Orpheus, Thomas Taylor
  (Bertram Dobbel)
New Larousse Encyclopedia of Mythology (Hamlyn
  Publishing)
The Persian Mystics, Abdullah Ansari (John
  Murray)
Pythagoras, Thomas Stanley (Philosophical
  Research Society)
The Questions of King Milinda, T. W. Rhys Davids
  (trans.) (Motilal)
The Quest of the Holy Grail, Pauline Matarasso
  (trans.) (Penguin)
The Quran, A. Yusuf Ali (trans.) (Islamic Center)
The Secret Doctrine, H. P. Blavatsky (Theosophical
  Univ. Press)
The Songs of Kabir, Rabindranath Tagore (trans.)
  (Weiser)
The Spiritual Guide, Michael Molinos (Christian
  Books)
The Sufis, Idries Shah (Doubleday)
Tales of the Mystic East, Singh (R. S. Satsang)
Tao Te Ching, Ch'u Ta-Kao (trans.) (Weiser)
Thus Spake Zarathustra, Freidrich Nietzsche
  (Macmillan)
Thrice Greatest Hermes, G. R. S. Mead (Weiser)

The Tibetan Book of the Dead, Fremantle &
  Trungpa (trans.) (Shambhala)
The Upanisads, Muller (trans.) (Dover)
*Views from the Real World: Early Talks with
  Gurdjieff*, (Dutton)
The Way of Zen, Alan Watts (Pantheon Books)
The White Goddess, Robert Graves (Farrar, Strauss,
  & Giroux)
Yoga Sutras of Patanjali, Charles Johnston (trans.)
  (Watkins)

MAGICK AND THE GODS

Book IV, Aleister Crowley (Weiser)
The Book of Pleasure, A. O. Spare (93 Publishing)
The Book of the Sacred Magic of Abramelin,
  Mathers (trans.) (de Laurence)
The Equinox, Vol. I nos. 1–10, Aleister Crowley
  (Weiser)
The Equinox, Vol. III no. 10, Aleister Crowley et al.
  (Weiser)
*Giordano Bruno and the Hermetic Tradition,
  Frances A. Yates (University of Chicago Press)
The Goetia, Aleister Crowley (ed.) (Magickal
  Childe)
History of Magic, Eliphas Levi (Weiser)
*Liber Aleph, Aleister Crowley (Weiser)
Magic and Mystery in Tibet, Alexandra David-Neel
  (Penquin)
Magic: The Western Tradition, Francis King (Avon
  Books)
Magick Without Tears, Aleister Crowley (New
  Falcon Publishing)
Magick in Theory and Practice, Aleister Crowley
  (Magickal Childe)
The Master Game, Robert S. DeRopp (Dell
  Publishing)
Man, Myth and Magic (24 Vols.) (Marshal
  Cavendish Corp.)
The Mirror of Magic, Kurt Seligmann (Pantheon
  Books)
Principles of Personal Defense, Jeff Cooper,
  (Wisdom Publishing)
Psychic Self Defense, Dion Fortune (Weiser)
Ritual Magic in England, Francis King (Neville
  Spearman)
Transcendental Magic, Éliphas Lévi (Weiser)

SECRET SOCIETIES

*Commentaries on the Holy Books, Aleister
  Crowley (Weiser)

The Devils of Loudon, Aldous Huxley (Harper &
  Row)

Divine Horsemen, Maya Deren (Dell)

Don Juan series, Carlos Casteneda (Simon &
  Schuster)

Down There (Là Bas), J. K. Huysmans (University
  Books)

An Encyclopedia of Freemasonry, (2 vols.) Albert
  Mackey (The Masonic History Company)

The Esoteric Orders and Their Work, Dion Fortune
  (Llewelyn)

*The Essential Golden Dawn: An Introduction to
  High Magic, Chic and Sandra Tabatha Cicero
  (Llewelyn)

Fire in the Minds of Men, James H. Billington (Basic
  Books)

Freemasonry, W. Kirk MacNulty (Thames and
  Hudson)

The Golden Builders, Tobias Churton (Weiser)

*The Golden Dawn, (2 vols.) Israel Regardie
  (Llewelyn)

*The Golden Dawn System of Magic, Israel
  Regardie (New Falcon)

*The Gnostic Philosphy, Tobias Churton (Inner
  Traditions)

The Great Seal of the United States, Paul Foster
  Case (J. F. Rowny Press)

The History of Freemasonry, Albert Mackey
  (Gramercy Books)

The Knights Templar, Stephen Howarth (Collins)

The Magical Revival, Kenneth Grant (Weiser)

*The Nag Hammadi Library, Robinson (ed.)
  (Harper & Row)

*The Origins of the Mithraic Mysteries, Ulansey
  (Oxford)

*Parzival, Wolfram Von Eschenbach (Vintage)

The Rose Cross and the Age of Reason, Christopher
  McIntosh (Brill)

Rosicrucian Enlightenment, Frances A. Yates
  (Routledge)

The Rosicrucians, Christopher McIntosh (Weiser)

Satanism and Witchcraft, Jules Michelet (Citadel
  Press)

Secret Societies, Norman Mackenzie (Crescent
  Books)

*The Secret Teachings of All Ages, Manly P. Hall
  (Philosophical Research Society)

The Slaves Shall Serve: Mediations on Liberty,
  James Wasserman (Sekmet Books)

The Templars and the Assassins: The Militia of
  Heaven, James Wasserman (Inner Traditions)

*Zanoni, Edward Bulwer Lytton (Joseph Knight)

The Two Great Seals of the United States, Robert
  Hieronimus (Savitriaum)

SEXUALITY

The Pillow Book, Douglas & Slinger (Destiny)

The Encircled Serpent, M. Oldfield Howey
  (Richmond)

Eros and Evil, R. E. L. Masters (Julian Press)

Erotic Spirituality, Alan Watts (Collier)

The Great Mother, Erich Neumann (Princeton Univ.
  Press)

The Heart of the Goddess, Hallie Iglehart Austen
  (Wingbow)

*The Hebrew Goddess, Raphael Patai (KTAV
  Publishing)

*Hebrew Myths, Robert Graves & Raphael Patai
  (Doubleday)

Kama Sutra, Sir Richard Burton (trans.) (Inner
  Traditions)

Sexual Secrets, Douglas & Slinger (Destiny)

Sexual Symbolism, Knight & Wright (Julian Press)

*Sky Dancer, Keith Dowman (Routledge)

Taoist Secrets of Love, Mantak Chia (Aurora Press)

*XXXI Hymns to the Star Goddess, Frater Achad
  (93 Publishing)

ALCHEMY

Alchemy, Titus Burchkhardt (Stuart & Watkins)

Alchemy, Johannes Fabricus (Aquarian Press)

Alchemy & Mysticism, Alexander Roob (Taschen)

Alchemy: The Secret Art, Stanislas Klossowski de
  Rola (Avon)

Atalanta Fugiens, Michael Maier (Phanes Press)

A Collection of Emblems, George Wither (Scolar
  Press)

The Golden Game, Stanislas Klossowski de Rola
  (Braziller)

*The Phoenix, Manly P. Hall (Philosophical
  Research Society)

Robert Fludd, Joscelyn Godwin (Phanes Press)
Splendor Solis, Salomon Trismosin (Phanes Press)
Splendor Solis, Salomon Trismosin (Yogi
  Publications)

TAROT

The Book of Thoth, Aleister Crowley (Weiser)
The Book of Tokens, Paul Foster Case (Builders of
  the Adytum)
The Encyclopedia of Tarot, Stuart R. Kaplan (U.S.
  Games)
An Introduction to the Golden Dawn Tarot, Robert
  Wang (Weiser)
The Qabalistic Tarot, Robert Wang (Weiser)
Pictorial Key to the Tarot, Arthur Edward Waite
  (Weiser)
Tarot, Paul Foster Case (Macoy)
The Tarot, Sylvie Simon (Inner Traditions)
Tarot and Astrology, Muriel Bruce Hasbrouck
  (Destiny)

SYMBOLIST AND VISIONARY ART

Art and the Occult, Rachleff & Singer (Cromwell
  Editions)
Leonardo da Vinci, Patrice Boussel (Tabard Press)
The Marriage of Heaven and Hell, William Blake
  (Oxford)
The Mystic Spiral: Journey of the Soul, Jill Purce
  (Avon)
Pagan Mysteries in the Renaissance, Edgar Wind
  (Faber & Faber)
Post-Impressionists, Guy Cogeval (Chartwell
  Books)
Raphael, Jean-Pierre Cuzin (Konecky & Konecky)
Secrets of the Occult, C. A. Burland (Ebury Press)
Secret Symbolism in Occult Art, Fred Gettings
  (Harmony Books)
William Blake, Robin Hamlyn and Michael Phillips
  (Harry N. Abrams, Inc., Publishers)

ILLUSTRATION PERMISSIONS

PAGE ii: British Library, London

PAGE vi: Museo Xul Solar © Fundación Pan Klub — Buenos Aires, Argentina

PAGE viii: The Pierpont Morgan Library/Art Resource, NY

PAGE 3: Harry Price Collection, University of London, Mary Evans Picture Library

ASTROLOGY AND COSMOLOGY

PAGE 4: NASA (Hubble Telescope, photo by Don Figer)

PAGE 7: Studio 31

PAGE 9: Musée Conde, Chantilly

PAGES 10–11: Biblioteca Estense, Modena

PAGE 13: Pierpoint Morgan Library, NY, Morgan Beatus, M644, fol. 87 M644, f.87

PAGE 14: British Museum, London

PAGE 15: TOP, Studio 31

PAGE 16: TOP, Philosophical Research Society, Los Angeles

PAGE 18: Musée Conde, Chantilly

PAGE 19: British Library, HIP/Art Resource, NY

KABBALAH AND THE TREE OF LIFE

PAGE 20: Philosophical Research Society

PAGE 21: Philosophical Research Society

PAGE 24: Bibliothèque Nationale, Paris, Ms. hebr 1181, fol. 264 verso

PAGE 25: Biblioteca Nazionale Centrale di Forenze, illum. ms., fol. 114v

PAGE 26: LEFT, Copyright © 1955, 1997 Inkweed Graphics/Lionel Ziprin. Photo by Rick Young

PAGE 27: Harry Smith Archives. Photo by Don Snyder

PAGE 29: BOTTOM, Steffi Grant, *The Hidden Lore*

PAGE 30: *The Egyptian Book of the Dead*, Copyright © 1994, 1998 by James Wasserman

PAGE 31: photo by Ira Landgarten

PAGE 32: Victoria & Albert Museum, London #1689-1855

PAGE 33: Bayerische Staatsbibliothek, Munich

INITIATION

PAGE 34: Philosophical Research Society

PAGE 39: Academia, Venice

PAGE 40: British Museum, London

PAGE 41: Princeton Architectural Press, NY

PAGES 42–43: TOP, Inner Traditions

PAGE 44: TOP, Metropolitan Museum, NY

PAGE 44: BOTTOM, Oriental Institute, University of Chicago, A 27903

PAGE 45: Inner Traditions

PAGES 46–47: TOP, Birmingham Art Museum, England

PAGE 46: BOTTOM, Bibliotech Royale Albert I–MS Brussels 9246, fol. 2

PAGE 47: BOTTOM, Yale University

PAGE 48: Prado, Madrid

PAGE 49: Musée du Louvre

PAGE 51: The Frick Collection, NY

PAGE 52: TOP, Warburgh Institute, London

PAGE 52: BOTTOM, Weiser Publishing, NY

PAGE 53: Steffi Grant, *The Hidden Lore*

MAGICK AND THE GODS

PAGE 54: Private Collection

PAGE 58: TOP, British Museum, London, Papyrus #9901

PAGE 58: BOTTOM, Carlsberg Glyptotek, Copenhagen

PAGE 59: BOTTOM, Inner Traditons

PAGE 61: Indian Tourist Board

PAGE 62: University of Chicago Press, photo by Ogden Goelet

PAGE 63: Ordo Templi Orientis. Photo by Rick Young

PAGE 64: Kenneth and Steffi Grant

PAGE 67: Steffi Grant, *The Hidden Lore*

PAGE 69: Ordo Templi Orientis

SECRET SOCIETIES

PAGE 70: Photo by Illia Tulloch

PAGE 71: *Les Illuminés de Bavière et la Franc-Maçonnerie Allemande*, René Le Forestier, 1914

PAGE 75: *Shanar: Dedication Ritual of a Buryat Shaman in Siberia*, Virlana Tkacz, Sayan Zhambalov, and Wanda Phipps © Yara Arts Group 2002, Parabola Books, New York, 2002. Photo by Alexander Khantaev

PAGE 76: Réunion des Musées Nationaux/Art Resource, NY

PAGE 77: TOP, British Library, London. Photo credit HIP/Art Resource, NY

PAGE 77: BOTTOM, Private collection. Photo by Antiqua, Inc., Woodland Hills, CA

ABOUT THE AUTHOR

Photo by Illia Tulloch

JAMES WASSERMAN is a lifelong student of religion and spiritual development. After attending Antioch College, he spent several years studying with various teachers of meditation and other disciplines. Settling in New York in 1973, he began working at Samuel Weiser's, then the world's largest esoteric bookstore. In 1977, he left to found Studio 31, specializing in book production and graphic design.

In 1976, he joined Ordo Templi Orientis (O.T.O.), having explored Aleister Crowley's system of Scientific Illuminism. In 1979, he founded TAHUTI Lodge, the third oldest O.T.O. Lodge in the world. He played a key role in numerous seminal publications of the Crowley corpus. In addition to his work on the Thoth Tarot cards and *The Holy Books of Thelema*, his own book, *Aleister Crowley and the Practice of the Magical Diary*, first published in 1993, has been revised and expanded in a new edition.

He is also responsible for the widely acclaimed restoration of the Papyrus of Ani, *The Egyptian Book of the Dead: The Book of Going Forth by Day* published by Chronicle Books in 1994.

The Templars and the Assassins: The Militia of Heaven was published in 2001. Already translated into six languages, it is well on its way to becoming a modern classic.

The Slaves Shall Serve: Meditations on Liberty was published in 2004. This is his most controversial book. It provides an insightful analysis of the modern descent into collectivism and suggests steps to reclaim individual freedom.

He lives in New York with his wife and two children.

For more information, please visit:
www.jameswassermanbooks.com

BOOKS OF RELATED INTEREST

The Templars and the Assassins
The Militia of Heaven
by James Wasserman

Surrealism and the Occult
Shamanism, Magic, Alchemy, and the Birth of an Artistic Movement
by Nadia Choucha

Lords of Light
The Path of Initiation in the Western Mysteries
by W. E. Butler

The Hermetic Tradition
Symbols and Teachings of the Royal Art
by Julius Evola

The Secret History of Freemasonry
Its Origins and Connection to the Knights Templar
by Paul Naudon

Mary Magdalene, Bride in Exile
by Margaret Starbird

Secret Societies of America's Elite
From the Knights Templar to Skull and Bones
by Steven Sora

Founding Fathers, Secret Societies
Freemasons, Illuminati, Rosicrucians, and the Decoding of the Great Seal
by Robert Hieronimus, Ph.D.

INNER TRADITIONS • BEAR & COMPANY
P.O. Box 388
Rochester, VT 05767
1-800-246-8648
www.InnerTraditions.com

Or contact your local bookseller